Advance Praise for *Daring to Fight*

"I first met Victoria at a book launch signing for one of Michael Hyatt's new books, *Living Forward*.

As we stood there in line waiting to get our books signed, we struck up a conversation that would change both of our lives forever.

I immediately observed that Victoria was truly genuine. As she began to share more of her story, I realized that I was standing in front of someone who had overcome tremendous obstacles and raging storms.

In fact, not only did she survive, but Victoria thrived in her life and business because of her willingness to Dare to Fight. She is the perfect example of showing someone who is struggling with depression and anxiety how to stand on their own two feet and truly fight for their healing and health.

If you or someone you know is facing silent shame or struggling in silence, please give them this book and remind them they are not alone. Victoria has been there and she is ready to lead the way and walk alongside you to help you heal and fight your way to freedom."

Dr. Jevonnah "Lady J" Ellison
Certified Leading Master Coach
Founder, The Thrive Summit
Creator, The Thrive Mastermind

"Scripture holds a lot of healing power, but sometimes we need more than a simple, 'I'll pray for you' or 'Just have more faith.' In the throws of deep depression, sometimes you need someone to sit by you, reminding you of your worth. Our worth in God's eyes never changes. *Daring to Fight* gives concrete, illuminating insight into the world of deep depression and how this woman of God pulled herself out of the abyss and into leading others into the light as they traverse this rocky and lonely road."

– Joanne F. Miller
Author of *Creating a Haven of Peace*

"From the moment I saw Victoria sitting on the coach … in her jeans and work boots typing out a story for a small bible study, I knew there was a book fighting to come out. Watching from the sidelines as she has fought through the fears with courage and shared her story on paper has been captivating. The words in *Daring to Fight* give us all hope that the darkness can give way to light and shine beauty in the most difficult places."

– Teresa McCloy
Coach, Speaker, and Creator of the REALIFE Process

"Victoria approaches the topic of depression in a way that incorporates her own experience and faith that is refreshing. Her willingness to be vulnerable about her own struggles encourages readers to embark on their own journey towards healing with determination and perseverance. This book will challenge readers to face depression head-on, while also resting in the grace of God as they walk from darkness to light."

– Kim Avery, MA
Author of *The Prayer Powered Entrepreneur*

"*Daring to Fight* starts a conversation that is much needed in the church as mental health becomes a prominent issue in our society. Victoria is the ideal person to initiate this conversation since she openly shares her own struggles and graciously challenges others through that experience. She handles this topic with care as one who has been there and is now committed to encouraging others in their fight for freedom. Anyone who reads her story, whether struggling with depression or not, will definitely be challenged and inspired."

– Kent Julian, CSP
www.KentJulian.com

"As someone who's personally battled depression for years, I can say one thing, *Daring To Fight* is a timely and much-needed book. Too many live in shame when facing dark seasons, which makes it difficult to let people in, the one thing that would help them not feel like they are battling this fight alone. Well-meaning friends give their best advice but many times what is lacking is practical guidance that can point people in the right direction. In *Daring To Fight*, my friend, Victoria Mininger lays out a blueprint for what it takes to battle depression head-on with grit, grace, and faith from a strong foundation in God's Word to intentional rhythms. This book is a must-read for anyone facing dark seasons."

– Csilla Muscan
Speaker and Author of *Finding Your Voice*,
www.csillamuscan.com

"*Daring to Fight* is not only a book about courage, but a book of courage providing hope and insight in dealing with the realities of depression and ambition. Victoria doesn't hide her emotions and bravely shares the self-talk she utilized along the journey; allowing us to see how she embraced God's plan for her in overcoming the many challenges in her life. Her vulnerability and real-ness in sharing her life lessons made the book engaging and hard to put down."

– Jeff McManus
Author of *Growing Weeders into Leaders*

Daring
to
Fight

Daring to Fight

When Grit, Grace & Faith
Take Depression Head-On

Victoria Mininger

NASHVILLE

NEW YORK • LONDON • MELBOURNE • VANCOUVER

Daring to Fight

When Grit, Grace, & Faith Take Depression Head On

Published in New York, New York, by Morgan James Publishing. Morgan James is a trademark of Morgan James, LLC. www.MorganJamesPublishing.com

ISBN 9781631950667 paperback
ISBN 9781631950674 eBook
Library of Congress Control Number: 2020933312

Cover Design by: Chris Treccani, 3dogcreative.net

Interior Design by: Melissa Farr, melissa@backporchcreative.com

Author Photo by: Gordon Dimming

Scripture quotations marked (NIV) are taken from the Holy Bible, New International Version®, NIV®. Copyright © 1973, 1978, 1984, 2011 by Biblica, Inc.™ Used by permission of Zondervan. All rights reserved worldwide. www.zondervan.com The "NIV" and "New International Version" are trademarks registered in the United States Patent and Trademark Office by Biblica, Inc.™

Scripture quotations marked (ESV) are from the ESV® Bible (The Holy Bible, English Standard Version®), copyright © 2001 by Crossway Bibles, a publishing ministry of Good News Publishers. Used by permission. All rights reserved.

Scripture quotations marked (NLT) are taken from the Holy Bible, New Living Translation, copyright ©1996, 2004, 2015 by Tyndale House Foundation. Used by permission of Tyndale House Publishers, a Division of Tyndale House Ministries, Carol Stream, Illinois 60188. All rights reserved.

Disclaimer: The information provided in this book is designed to give helpful information on the subjects discussed. This book is not meant to be used, nor should it be used, to diagnose or treat any medical condition. For diagnosis or treatment of any medical problem, consult your own physician or professional counselor. The author is not responsible for any specific health needs that may require medical supervision and is not liable for any damages or negative consequences from any treatment, action, application, or preparation, to any person reading or following the information in this book. References are provided for informational purposes only and do not constitute endorsement of any websites or other sources. Readers should be aware that the websites listed in this book may change.

Some names and identifying details have been changed to protect the privacy of individuals.

Morgan James is a proud partner of Habitat for Humanity Peninsula and Greater Williamsburg. Partners in building since 2006.

Get involved today! Visit
MorganJamesPublishing.com/giving-back

To Brian, Michaela, Anna, Rachel and Kaitlyn
You believed in me, even when I couldn't.

Contents

Acknowledgments

Writing a book is a daunting task. Doing so with your heart wide open is another matter entirely. To my husband, Brian, who saw this book before it was even written. Who believed in me even when I didn't believe in myself. You lifted me up when I was lying shattered on the ground and loved me anyways. For my girls who loved me at my best and made me smile at my worst, for you I am grateful. It was for each of you that I dared to fight for brighter days.

For my counselor, Lynn, who helped me put on my fighting gloves and coached me as I stepped into the ring. Every time I didn't think I could go on, you were there to help me fight another day. God brought you into my life at just the right time. For that I am thankful.

To my mom and dad, who taught me how to fight forward and dig in with grit until I made it to the other side.

To my mom-in-law who was a prayer warrior on my behalf. Indeed, the prayers of a righteous person avail much.

To those who coached me along the way as I got back up on my feet, who championed me as I began to lead again. You helped me to rise well.

For my friend, Teresa McCloy, who challenged me to just start writing and see what God wanted to do, and to Nick Pavlidis for cheering me on to start this book and helping me navigate the beginning steps of bringing this book to life.

To the Morgan James Publishing family for believing in this book and helping me navigate all the ins and outs of bringing this book to the world, especially David Hancock, Jim Howard, Bethany Marshall, and Bonnie Rauch.

For my editor, Aubrey Kosa, and your diligence to make sure I crossed all my Ts and dotted all my Is. Without you, this book would still be sitting in my computer with way too many run-on sentences and poor grammar. You are an amazing and talented woman.

And to all those who dare to fight the darkness of depression. This book is for you. Remember, you never travel alone.

Foreword

If you find yourself with this book in your hands, it is not a mistake; it is not happenstance. It is a divine intervention. The God of the universe sees your pain. He is pursuing you and seeking to make you whole.

> *"And the God of all grace ... after you have suffered a little while, will himself restore you and make you strong, firm and steadfast."* (1 Peter 5:10, NIV).

You have suffered a little while, and now God has determined it is the time for you to become strong, firm, and steadfast. Sadness is loss. Depression is hopelessness. To varying degrees, we all experience this. When you believe things are hopeless, your body and your brain take you into a depressive state to protect you from the continual pain of a shattered dream. God Himself is seeking to restore you and replace your shattered dream. Through *Daring to Fight*, Victoria will powerfully comfort you with the comfort she has received (2 Cor 1:4 NIV).

Many of you will never have the privilege of meeting Victoria. I remember meeting her when she was bruised and beaten, fighting through the confusion and haze that is depression. This is not a book written by a dry "professional" who personally has never been through this kind of fight. This is not a book written by a counselor who has never actually experienced depression. This is a book written by a fighter, a conqueror in Jesus who has personally fought and overcome depression and anxiety. If you take these pages seriously, you will find freedom. Fight the good fight. Be bold and courageous, just as Victoria was. Throw off everything that hinders, including the lie of hopelessness. Because hopelessness was abolished on the cross of Jesus Christ.

Lynn Schwenk, M.A., LPC
Restoration Counseling

CHAPTER I

Victoria's Story

I remember as if it was yesterday. Light streamed in through the living room windows, lighting the space inside our home. I could hear my husband quietly moving around: washing dishes, starting a load of laundry, feeding the dogs, and putting them out for the day. The children were already on the school bus, yet another task he had attended to earlier that morning. Patiently, quietly, he moved from one room to the next as I lied there on the couch. While I could see the light coming through the window and feel its warmth, the sun's rays struggled to pierce the darkness that seemed to fill my world.

It had been three months of lying there on that couch, drifting in and out of sleep, struggling to push through the long hours of the day. Nights felt even longer. The days passed like a silent black and white film on repeat. Very little seemed to pierce the grayness of those hours. As I look back, I can so vividly see myself lying there, as if I were an outside observer, seeing my physical body from an outside space. For a brief moment, I feel sad for her. That shell of a woman I used to know. A woman who had taken on too much with too little margin. Whose heart longed to serve, but broke under the weight of it all.

It's funny how depression comes sneaking in. Months prior to my time on the couch, I would have never imagined myself in such a place of hopelessness and despair. Living in a world gray and unfeeling. Looking back, my depression had been building for a long time. But just as an earthquake can hit without warning, so did the darkness.

Into the Darkness

It was early November, and I was painting a house. I often picked up side work to help make ends meet for our growing family of six, while my husband worked as a pastor along with a full-time job at a construction company forty-five minutes away.

I had been painting this house for weeks. First the front, than each side, followed by the back of the house. Finally, only one corner remained, accessed by a low shed roof that sloped towards the ground only feet below.

As I stood on that roof, rhythmically painting one board after another, I listened to the quiet of the woods that surrounded the low-slung country farmhouse. It was a house that I had come to intimately know from weeks of painting the same box. The birds called to each other, as if to declare that winter was not yet here with its icy grip. Yet, I was already feeling the chill of something bigger than winter deep inside.

The truth was, those days of painting gave me a lot of thinking time. The last ten years of life had taken their toll. The start of the deeper struggle was losing our business to bankruptcy during the 2009 housing crash. It was a blow that few saw coming, and we were unprepared for it like so many others. Just months before the crash we had we relocated our family to a beautiful mountainous town about forty-five minutes outside our hometown. We were answering what we had discerned as, along with our church leadership, a call to pastor a small church plant in that area. This pastoral call had come to us two years prior to the crash, when our business was thriving and supporting us well as a family. The original plan was to support ourselves with our business while planting this new church. It seemed that God was orchestrating the perfect plan for us to run our business and pursue this ministry call. But it was not to be. Instead, we started our first years of church planting on shaky ground as we tried to process the extreme loss of our business, altered relationships, and what felt like a darkened reputation in our previous community. Those were hard years, ones with a lot of questions from ourselves and from people who didn't understand the magnitude of our loss. Their harsh criticism of my husband and the ongoing gossip about our failed business weighed heavy, even though my husband did his best to shield me from the cutting words of others. Now, like so many, we were looking for work in a hurting economy, struggling to rebuild a life in a new place, and, at times, questioning God in it all.

Besides the loss of our business, I was also trying to figure out my new role as a pastor's wife, working to get a small business off the ground, finding my footing in a new community, and mothering our four little girls without the help of family, who had always been nearby. All the while, I was hoping and praying to build meaningful and healthy friendships with the women around me. Those first years in a new place were hard and full of firsts. There was so much to focus on and tackle, but I felt up to the task and wanted to do all of it—well.

On the Enneagram personality test, I fall squarely in line as a two. Twos are helpers by nature and, being an Enneagram two, my natural helper personality was fitting for all the roles I was trying to fill in that season. I didn't know it then, but I've since come to find out that my helper personality, while it can be my superpower, can very much be my kryptonite. I grew up on a dairy farm in northern New Mexico. And, like any farm, there is always work to do. From an early age, my parents taught me the value of hard work. If there was something to be done, you did it until it was finished. And my little Enneagram-two self thrived on getting stuff done and helping others. My heart ate up the praise that came from doing and helping. I loved when my parents received compliments on my helping behavior. Oh how I would shine at that praise.

Fast-forward to my adult years, where hard work was still important, in particular for a pastor's wife, fledgling business owner, and mom of four. There were always things to do, roles to fill, and people to serve. Honestly, my heart thrived in that place—until one day it didn't.

Somewhere in all that "hard work" and "doing," I forgot the most important thing. When you work hard, you also have to rest well. But I don't think I knew how to do that. Nobody questioned whether I had hard work down pat. I had always been known as the one to get things done and done well. That wasn't my problem. My problem was not in the doing but in the being. It was not in the starting of something as much as the stopping of something. Of learning the value of saying "no" instead of a never-ending stream of "yes." Somewhere along the line, I had severely neglected resting well, and I was about to pay a hefty price for remaining blind for too long to the strain "yes" can put on a body.

But I found "no" hard to dole out, especially to those closest to me like my husband. When we married in 1996, I stood up in front of 250 witnesses on our wedding day and committed to love him and serve alongside him for the rest of our days. I had also stood up in front of our home congregation just a few years prior, when they commissioned us to the work of church planting, and I promised to be his helpmate in this ministry. I did not take these promises lightly and I intended to fill them with love, honor, integrity, and hard work. I was up for the challenge…or so I thought.

The truth is, whether you are running a business, planting a church, or raising a family, there is always more work to be done than hands to help. So every time there was a ministry need that needed extra hands or a side job came up that could use my help or the girls' school just needed one more batch of cookies, guess whose hand went up in the air. Every. Single. Time. Looking back, I swear my arm was on one of those pendulum ball sets that you set on your desk to keep time. It's fascinating to watch but a brutal roller coaster to stay on. That kind of roller coaster is where life found me that cold November day as I painted a house. One long brush stroke after another, I reflected on all the times I had handed out a "yes." The list was staggering, and I knew deep down that this pace I had been running and this load I had been carrying were not sustainable.

But it would take the slow, rhythmic strokes of painting a house to finally bring me to that point of honesty.

That day in November, I was finally ready to admit to myself that I couldn't carry the weight of all the tasks and commitments on my shoulders any longer. The reality became apparent to me. I was so out of balance that it wouldn't take much to push me over the edge. The truth, that now so boldly stared me in the face and that I had worked so hard to ignore, was that if I didn't drop everything right then and there, I wasn't sure I would be alive the next year.

That realization was a scary and painful one for me. I had so much to live for, yet the life I was leading was one I could no longer manage on my own. In that moment, on that roof, I knew what I had to do. I couldn't pretend any longer for myself or for anyone else. Enough was enough. I set my paintbrush down on top of the open paint can, pulled out my phone, and dialed my husband. I knew he was probably on a job site somewhere and might not be able to pick up the call. His workload was often heavy, and the demands on his time frequent. Part of me was desperate to hear his voice; the other part just wanted to run. It rang once, twice, and then his voice broke through.

"Hey Hon, how's the painting going?" my husband said as he answered.

"I'm done!" I declared.

"Wow, great!" He enthusiastically responded. Getting this job done meant we could finally pay the gas bill that had been looming over our heads.

I paused, a bit frustrated that he didn't catch my immediate meaning. With a bit of a panicked voice, I uttered, *"No, you don't understand. I'm still painting, but I'm done. I'm done juggling everything. I'm done. Really done. I can't do it anymore. The church stuff. The business stuff. The house stuff. Everything. I'm done. I can't do this anymore, and as of right now, I am dropping it all."* I paused before continuing, *"I have to, or I'm not sure where I'll be next year, Hon."*

The air between the lines hung with a palpable silence. Honestly, I wasn't sure if this declaration would surprise my husband or not. For the last two years, we had often talked about how weary I was beginning to feel and how heavy the load was getting. We had spent hours walking around the cow fields at home, going back and forth about how to juggle this and that. Often our discussions ended in frustration as he failed to see my weariness and I failed to speak clearly what was in my heart. The reality was that he was feeling just as weary as I was. He was working long hours to provide for our family and shepherd a small church. He was also still working to process the years of loss prior to our move and trying to find some solid footing for himself. There just was not enough room for me to not be okay. He needed me to be okay so that he could focus on those other areas that were important too. But the day I called him from that shed roof was the day the harsh reality began to hit both of us that I was far from okay anymore.

It's funny the things you can remember about a day. Have you ever had a moment that just etches itself in your brain? Sounds, smells, thoughts, and feelings. So poignant that the very memory of them makes you startle. Moments that years later seem as clear as the day you experienced them. That phone call to my husband is such a memory for me.

I feel the hesitation in my body just before I dare pick up the phone, my shaking fingers somehow dialing the familiar phone number. And that panicked moment when my brain said run and yet my heart knew that this pivotal moment might never happen again. Then the pause, and then a long press of the button, and, as it rings, practicing the words that seem so hard to get out. Words that, in essence, will say, "I can't go on. Help me. Love me. Don't leave me."

In that moment, admitting to him that I was not okay was hard for me to do. I wanted to be strong for him. I wanted to shoulder the weight of life together and to be the best partner in marriage and life that I could be. But as hard as it was for me to admit that I was not okay, I realized much later that it was just as hard for him to hear. A few years later, after the worst of my depression had lifted, he would share with me that he was so caught up in taking care of everyone else that somehow he missed caring for the most important person in his life. My phone call that day shook him to his core, and he realized that much of the weight I was bearing was a result of him allowing it to rest on my shoulders. Guilt weighed heavy on him for years as I bore the brunt of, in his words, "what he had done to me and allowed to be put upon me."

Breaking into the silence I continued shakily, *"Honey, I realize this is not what you signed up for. When you married me and asked me to serve beside you in ministry, I was all in, but now I can't go on anymore. So, if that means you need to walk away from our marriage then, okay. I get it. I failed. I failed you, and I failed God. It's okay. I would completely understand. I'm sure you could find a better wife."*

And I waited. Waited with bated breath. Certain of his next words. In all honesty, I was fully prepared for him to walk away because, in my overwhelmed heart, my brain could only fathom one answer from him. The answer I felt I deserved for what I saw as my complete failure as a wife, mother, and ministry partner. And, in the waiting, I heard him catch his breath. Then he simply uttered these four words: *"Babe, I'm coming home."*

And in that moment, as he spoke those words, it was as if I could finally exhale all the doubt, pain, shame, and failure I felt. I could finally let go of everything on my plate and just be. He was voluntarily choosing to stay, and in that moment, it was as if God whispered, *"I'm not going anywhere either."*

You Are Not Alone

If you have picked up this book, my guess is that somewhere along the line you have struggled with depression or anxiety too. Across the many people I have sat with, exchanged messages with, or had conversations with, often it seems that depression and anxiety go hand in hand.

Maybe your depression battle is something that comes and goes, rising and falling with the season or life circumstances. Maybe you have been fighting for a long time. So long, in fact, that you can barely remember when it all started. No matter where you find yourself, I want you to know this one important truth: You are not alone. According to the World Health Organization, over 300 million people live with depression globally. Statistically speaking, one in four Americans will experience depression at some point in their lives.[i] Those numbers are staggering and growing every day, across every age group, gender, profession, financial status, and demographic.

However, if you are like me, all those statistics can just feel like numbers rather than actual people. And numbers still keep us feeling very much alone and isolated. When I was working through my own depression, I found that the isolation I faced seemed due, in part, to the depression I faced. This was partially from a lack of understanding and resources and partly from the conversation about depression remaining hushed in many families, groups, and churches today. You mention depression, and the room grows quiet. People don't know what to say and often look like they might want to run for their lives. And I get it. Talking about depression can make us feel uncomfortable and leave us searching for words, and this is coming from someone who has experienced it, worked through it, and found her way to the other side. There are still times when I facilitate a support group for depression and am left without words. Because, honestly, sometimes there are no words.

However, I do believe that the tide is changing. We are starting to hear rumblings of conversation, raised awareness, and people who are brave enough to step to the forefront of that conversation. And in having conversation, hopefully action can continue so that we can offer better care for those who struggle with depression and other mental health challenges. That is why it is so important that we continue these conversations ourselves. That is why I have chosen to write this book and to push through the discomfort and the tension that comes with tough conversations like this. If my voice, added to the chorus of voices that is beginning to rise, can help others know that they are not alone in their struggles, then I will bravely venture forward, battling through the embarrassment and shame that so quickly wants to take hold of my heart and push me back into oppressive isolation. It is worth the fight.

Because shame wants to do those things. It wants to pile up on our shoulders, daring us to give in to its lies. To bury us under the weight of its accusations and falsehoods. Shame tells us that we are not good enough, that there is something fundamentally wrong with us. That if we were just strong enough, we could just get over it already.

If you're a Christian believer, as I am, you may even hear whispers from well-meaning friends about your faith being somehow lacking. Did you feel it? The burden of shame just got heavier as we regale ourselves with these very same self-doubting thoughts. As much as we would like to get upset at others for saying such things, the truth is, we are already saying them to ourselves.

And yet, from my experience, depression and even anxiety are rarely just faith issues. The roots run much deeper than whether you have a strong or weak faith or any faith at all. Depression and anxiety are complex and cannot be fixed by just praying more, reading more scripture, or going to church another night of the week. Now, before you slam the book shut and cry "heresy," know that I am not saying those things are not important. In fact, I believe that God's Word and prayer are key in this battle against depression. However, what I have come to know, through my own dark struggle, is that to make forward progress against the grip of depression and anxiety, it also takes a lot of intentional work and steps towards health and healing.

In all honesty, during the worst of my depression battle, I was certain that I was simply too broken to be loved by anyone. The friends I thought would walk with me during the hard times of my life were all of the sudden very absent. I struggled to understand the silence. I struggled to process the pain that came from the abandonment. I struggled to know what to do with the anger that filled my body and drove me to a deep, two-year silence.

(In Chapter 4, we'll talk more about how to handle the disappointment and pain that occurs when others fail us and how sometimes those very friends may not be the people who can walk with you in this hard place.)

And while there will be those who, while they may not have walked your journey and may not fully understand, will choose to walk with you anyway, there are also those who do understand in a deeper way. People, like myself, who have journeyed as you are now. Others who have struggled in similar ways as you. How we got to this place of depression may look different, but there is a shared story in our pain. In fact, if you have walked very long in this place of depression, I can almost guarantee that you can look at someone and know when they are struggling. There is a look in their eyes that tells you of a deeper sorrow that goes beyond a bad day or a fleeting sadness. And you connect to that person not because your stories are exactly the same but because you know what it feels like to be in that place. It is in those connections that we find a commonality and a kinship—and come to know that we don't travel in this place alone.

However, I want to be really honest with you. One thing I can tell you about this depression battle is that while others can travel with you, they cannot do the work for you. They may want to because they care for you, but the reality is, they cannot pick up your pain and carry it for you. They cannot shoulder the darkness and see it through to the light. There comes a point when you will have to pick up your head, stand up on your feet, and take a step. You will have to own your story, no matter how messy it is, and start walking.

And the walking will be painful, possibly painful to the point that you'd rather stay camped out in depression valley. I almost built a house there, so I know the temptation to just remain. Even if it's painful, at least it's comfortable and you know what to expect, right? Because the truth is, when we begin to work through the things that may have triggered or led to our depression, our pain increases as we take steps to address the wounds deep in our hearts and minds. And yet, it's the only way I know through this dark valley. To lift your head, tilt your chin, and, with shaking fingers and shaking knees, say "yes" to taking those first steps–that first step when your brain is telling you to run, but your heart is telling you this pivotal moment matters and may never come again.

Despite the pain, what I do know is that as you start taking those steps, God himself will meet you there, if you will let Him. He may feel incredibly distant. You may be angry with Him for allowing this depression into your life. You may question everything you know about God or even doubt if He really exists at all. But that does not change the truth that I know. God has not left, nor will He ever leave you. He is ready as you begin to own your story.

Deuteronomy 31: 6 (ESV) says:
> "Be strong and courageous. Do not fear or be in dread of them, for it is the Lord your God who goes with you. He will not leave you or forsake you."

And then in Jeremiah 29:11 (NIV):
> "For I know the plans I have for you declares the Lord, plans to prosper you and not to harm you, plans to give you a hope and a future."

And can we just be honest? When you're battling depression or anxiety, Scripture can be hard to receive. Really, really hard. During my depression battle, I often felt like those promises of God were for everyone except me. You know what I mean? When you sit in church and the pastor is sharing truth and life through God's Word but the words feel hollow and instead choke your throat and tears seep from your eyes as you desperately try to grab hold of the words just out of your reach.

And yet, even then, God's Word is for you.

His promises are for you.

Even if right now you are struggling to believe his Word for yourself, know that he sees you and continues to love you just the same. I can imagine that maybe the people of Israel faced some of the same struggles.

Looking at the Deuteronomy verse, we see that this promise was spoken through Moses prior to the Israelites crossing the Jordan River into the Promised Land. But here was the clincher. The part that maybe you didn't know because maybe, like me, you hadn't heard the whole context of this scripture before. Within that Promised Land, there were still battles to be fought and enemies to be conquered. It was not going to be an easy journey into the Promised Land. It's *because* of the difficulties before them that God tells them to be strong and courageous, reassuring them that He would go before them and never, ever leave them.

The promise didn't come to them in good times or after they had conquered the land. It came before they had done any of the work, had fought any battles, forded any streams, or slayed any giants. (Yes, there were actual giants in the land, descendants of Anak. Crazy, I know!) But just like you and I, the Israelites were at the beginning of their fight for this land that God had promised them. So God brought them his word, his bond that He would never leave them nor forsake them. Because when you go into battle for anything worthwhile, there will be intense moments when you will question the truth of that promise. *"Really God? Really? I hope you were serious about that God because I really need to know you are there as I take this next hard step."*

And while it's true that as you embrace your story and begin to battle depression it will not be easy, I can also say with assurance that, as you seek the Lord, He will go before you.

Friend, it's time to be strong and courageous, to cross into the promise of hope and healing God offers as we battle forward.

This is truly where the "grit" part of the journey comes in. Every person has to determine that they are ready to fight. You have to decide that you have had enough and are ready to do what it takes to start walking forward. No one else can make that decision for you or take those first steps. They can encourage you and point you to resources, but they cannot do your work. That part is up to *you*.

And as you battle, be reminded that in Jeremiah 29:11 God says that He has a plan and purpose for your life. It is not over yet. There is so much more good to come, even if you are struggling to see it right now. When Jeremiah proclaimed this encouragement from God to the Jewish exiles, it was during a time of great turmoil. All they owned would be taken from them, and they had no idea if they would ever be free to return to their homes. It was not an easy time, and this promise that Jeremiah shared with the people was sent to encourage their hearts during a very discouraging time—a time when there seemed to be no hope for any kind of future.

Like you, I know what that hopelessness feels like. You wonder if life will ever be better. You wonder if you can ever feel normal again. You wonder if you'll ever stop crying, if life will hold any interest again, if the pain will ever get better.

My friend, that's why these verses are for you and me. They are to remind us that, even in the most hopeless of situations, in our greatest despair, there is hope for the future. And it starts with learning to own your own story.

Own Your Own Story

Owning our own stories can be hard. Often, when we find ourselves in a place of pain, we look around for someone to blame. We search for the simple answer for why we are where we are. Sometimes we refuse to take any steps forward because we are waiting for someone else to fix it. To fix the pain. To fix the circumstances. To apologize. To say they are truly sorry. To be repentant for what they have done to us. Or we hold on to our right to be angry because it at least allows us to feel something, right? Or maybe, we just sit there not knowing where to start but knowing we need to start somewhere.

Yet, as we linger and spin in that space, we never actually make any forward progress. At some point, we have to be willing to lean in to the discomfort of addressing our depression, of addressing the pain, of holding conversation with others, to take those beginning steps. Beginning steps that only *you* can take. And just like the phone call I made that day to my husband, I vividly remember my beginning steps in much the same way.

The day started like so many of the days before. Early morning sun spilled and played across the hardwood floors of our home. I passively watched as my dog yelped and chased the glimmers of light across the floor, she being utterly convinced that she would catch one today. The girls had been at school for at least an hour, so the house would be empty of their giggles and girlish chatter for the next couple of hours. My husband shuffled between the kitchen and our office, tending to who knows what, as I had lost track of what needed to be done. I can still feel that loose spring in the couch cushion, and how I shifted every day just enough to not feel it pressing into my hip.

As I was lying there, I remembered starting my daily conversation with God. By this point, I had my routine and our conversation down pat. A daily conversation that usually started with:

"Why?"
"I don't understand."
"Where is everybody?"
"Why has no one come?"
"God, I don't want to stay here. Help me!"

'Round and 'round I went in my head, uttering the same things. Desperation laced my inner thoughts while sighs punctuated the space around me. They were the same old questions that just never seemed to have any answers. Yet, I desperately wanted to hear. I desperately wanted help. I desperately wanted to get better.

But something was different that day. I really can't tell you what. Maybe it was that I refused to stop pounding on the door of heaven, or maybe after all the questions something was finally crystallizing in my mind. Looking back, I now know and believe that God Himself was breaking through the fog of my thoughts and confusion. As I paused between my questions, I had this seeming moment of clarity. Clarity that made me suddenly realize that no other human being was coming to my rescue. That the saving was not going to come from the people around me but from the God who had created me. If I was going to get off the couch and get better, I was going to have to take the first steps. I needed to figure this one out and do whatever it took to move forward.

Don't misunderstand me here. It's not that the people in my life didn't want to help me. They just did not know how. They didn't know where to start and felt just as lost as I did when it came to knowing what to do for me. It was in that moment of realizing that no one was coming to my rescue that I knew it was time to get real and honest with my own story and own up to it—to own the parts of my story that were mine to own. The places where I had failed and took on too much. I had to own that while other people had hurt me, if I waited for them to make things right, I might be waiting a long time. It was up to me to own my story, all the good, the bad, and the ugly of it. It was time for me to take my power back. It was time to stand up and dare to fight.

Did owning my story excuse the people in my life who had wounded me, intentionally or unintentionally? Absolutely not. However, owning my story was what would allow me to finally start taking the steps I needed to get better.

That morning, as this new realization hit me, I sat up, literally. I was going to go for a walk! It was time to take some literal steps. The time had come for me to get up, get off the couch, and dare to fight this depression that had taken over my life, no matter how slow that might be.

I remember slipping on my shoes and calling out to my husband. *"Brian, I'm going for a walk around the field."*

He popped his head around the corner, with a slightly surprised look on his face. However, like a wise husband, he only said, *"Okay, great. Want me to come along?"*

"No," I said. *"I'll be okay. I'm just going to get some fresh air."*

And that was my first step in owning my story— owning my story and declaring that enough was enough.

I was on a mission to get well. To get back to living life. I was daring to fight!

"*When we deny the story, it defines us.*
When we own the story, we can write a brave new ending."
— BRENÉ BROWN

Your Turn

1. Where does your story begin? Do you struggle to know that it matters? If so, why?

2. What parts of your story do you need to own?

3. Are you ready to take those first steps, to ask yourself the hard questions? If not, what do you think is holding you back?

4. What is one step you can take this week to own your story?

This Week's Activity

Following along with the first question, take time this week to write out your story. Don't worry if it's not neat and clean. Don't worry about grammar and sentence flow. Just write. No one will be reading it, and you don't have to share it with anyone. This is for you. Owning our stories starts with acknowledging that they exist and that they matter.

"I am bent, but not broken.
I am scarred, but not disfigured.
I am sad, but not hopeless.
I am tired, but not powerless.
I am angry, but not bitter.
I am depressed, but not giving up."

– AUTHOR UNKNOWN

CHAPTER 2

What is Depression?

You would think that, with a degree in psychology and counseling and my ongoing study of human behavior, it wouldn't have taken me so long to see and understand what was really happening inside me.

But, the reality is, it took me a long time to realize that I was actually in a serious battle with depression. For me, it was a gradual buildup over the course of two years, two years of doing too much for too long. Maybe because of its slow buildup, I failed to see how bad it was getting until it stared me blatantly in the face. Truthfully, depression was much easier to recognize in others than it was in myself. And maybe it wasn't that I didn't see it in myself as much as I wasn't ready to acknowledge that I saw it in myself. It's easier to acknowledge a struggle we see in another than to acknowledge that we might be facing a similar challenge.

Or maybe it was pride. Or hidden shame. Maybe it was denial.

Whatever the reason that it took me so long to see the depression in myself, once I realized what I was dealing with, I have to admit I spent a fair amount of time researching and trying to understand what was happening inside my head. I would analyze the information, picking or discarding things I thought applied or didn't. *"Hmmm. I seem to have this, but not that. Ongoing sadness? Yes. Loss of interest? Yes. Anger? Nope, not a problem."* Or so I thought.

Deep, internal anger was one of my strongest indicators, but it manifested as ongoing irritation, a short temper, and a sharp tongue. It wasn't until I sought out a counselor that I was able to see just how much anger had become a player in my depression story. It would take my counselor's outside perspective to help me address and conquer the anger that had been building for so long.

Before we go any further, let me say that I strongly believe it's important to understand what is happening in our own bodies and minds. No one can advocate for you better than you. That is true. However, while researching and knowing what is happening in your own body is important, I am not advocating for self-diagnosing and just winging it. What I *am* advocating for is a willingness to understand what is happening inside of you paired with healthy measures like seeing a qualified counselor and/or doctor for evaluation. We often cannot see our whole picture, such as when my counselor was able to point out the anger that had built up in my own life. That relationship with my counselor was vital for me to take strong steps towards healing and wholeness.

I'll talk more in Chapter 5 about doctors and counselors and the vital role they play in this battle against depression. For now, let's talk more about what depression is.

Some people may experience a mild depression or what is sometimes referred to as generalized depression. Many of the symptoms of depression are similar but maybe not as strong as what is seen in something like major depressive disorder. For reference, here is how major depressive disorder is defined by the American Psychiatric Association:

"Depression (major depressive disorder) is a common and serious medical illness that negatively affects how you feel, the way you think and how you act. Fortunately, it is also treatable. Depression causes feelings of sadness and/or a loss of interest in activities once enjoyed. It can lead to a variety of emotional and physical problems and can decrease a person's ability to function at work and at home."[ii]

Whether you suffer from generalized depression or major depressive disorder, symptoms of depression can vary from mild to severe and generally last longer than two weeks. While not everyone agrees on the exact list of symptoms, below are the ones most commonly listed across the board:

✦ Feeling sad or in an ongoing depressed mood
✦ Loss of interest in things you used to enjoy
✦ Restlessness
✦ Avoidance or isolation from normal relationships
✦ Ongoing irritation
✦ Changes in appetite, either overeating or eating very little
✦ Changes in mood from your normal personality
✦ Loss of energy or fatigue beyond what is normal
✦ Feelings of worthlessness
✦ Deep internal anger
✦ Physical complaints that seem to have no underlying medical reason
✦ Sleep changes
✦ Difficulty thinking or making decisions
✦ Thoughts of death or suicide

It's important to keep in mind that there are other types of medical conditions that can mimic the symptoms of depression, so it's important to rule out other possible medical issues with your doctor. Another key thing to remember is that depression affects our whole being: physical, emotional, mental, and spiritual. Depression is no respecter of persons and really does not care how much money you have in your bank account.

Depression affects men and women, children, and young adults and runs the gamut of age, from old to the very young. It bridges every socioeconomic status, every race and genre of people. According to the World Health Organization, "Depression is the leading cause of disability worldwide."[iii]

Sometimes depression can linger for a long time before you realize what's happening, such as was the case for me. Looking back, I now realize that I battled generalized depression starting in my late teens years going well into adulthood. Sometimes a family member or a close friend will recognize it in us, but they won't completely know what is going on either. I call depression "a master of disguises" because it can fly under the radar for a long time before being found out or triggered by events in your life.

It's important to realize that you may experience other symptoms than what I listed above or what you find in your own research. Since our bodies are all uniquely created, no one person is going to necessarily respond to depression the same way their friend or family member might. Elderly people may display symptoms differently than their younger counterparts and vice versa. That is why it's important to realize that one solution may not fit every single person. Medications or therapies that work for one person may not be effective for another.

Sometimes people who are battling depression don't seem sad at all. They may seem full of energy, laughing at everything, being the life of the party. Nothing is ever wrong, and they never have any problems. The reality may be that they are hurting deep inside. They simply deal with that hurt by masking it with their "over-the-top" exuberance. In the past, I would often mask my own pain with laughter and a false mask of happiness just to escape the discomfort of what was taking place inside.

We can also mask our depression through addictive behaviors like excessive drinking, drugs (either recreational or prescription), overeating, excessive shopping, hoarding, or even stress coping behaviors. These outward behaviors often manifest in an effort to mask and deal with the underlying feelings of depression and/or anxiety. Often when I was overtaxed and stressed, I turned to soda. Maybe that doesn't sound so bad to you, but for me, it became an addictive behavior because I was nursing my stress, hurts, and wounds with excessive sugar consumption instead of finding a healthier way to deal with my stress.

Causes of Depression

Today, researchers have come a long way in their understanding of depression and its causes. Since every person is unique, the causes of each person's depression can be varied and affected by a number of different factors.

Often there are multiple factors that affect a person's depression. According to the Harvard Health Review:

> "Research suggests that depression doesn't spring from simply having too much or too little of certain brain chemicals. Rather, there are many possible causes of depression, including faulty mood regulation by the brain, genetic vulnerability, stressful life events, medications, and medical problems. It's believed that several of these forces interact to bring on depression."[iv]

Let's look closer at some of these "forces" that may be taking place in our lives and contributing to or triggering depression.

Hereditary

Science has shown a hereditary disposition to certain things, such as medical issues and depression. Studies show that a person is more likely to struggle with depression if a close family member has struggled with depression. However, just because you might have a genetic predisposition to depression doesn't mean you will automatically struggle with it. I know that I have some hereditary disposition to depression in my family. For a long time, I was not aware of it, but I had conversations with family members that awakened me to this possible connection. Knowing this information made a difference in how my doctor and counselor handled my care and how I approach my own mental health today.

Environment

In this case, I'm not talking about the weather or saving the rainforest. Instead, when I reference environment, I am referring to your general surroundings at your home, place of work, and/or the communities you spend time with. If you live or work in a high-stress environment, where tension or unhealthy coping exist, be mindful that these factors can contribute to an underlying depression or build up over time. Who you surround yourself with and what type of environment you allow yourself to be influenced by matter. It's amazing to me how our environment can have such a strong influence in our lives–physically, emotionally, mentally, and spiritually.

Secondary

Although my depression was finally triggered by an overload of stress and work, I look back now and realize my depression was also impacted by other health factors, such as three pregnancies in less than five years. My twin pregnancy was especially difficult and the delivery traumatic, adding to the stress I already carried as a new mom of a toddler. A third pregnancy followed just two years later. Then I had two major surgeries—one for endometriosis, resulting in a partial hysterectomy, and a second major surgery to fix sinus problems from birth. Both the hysterectomy and sinus surgeries brought relief from years of pain and ongoing issues, but they also ushered in a load of physical, emotional, and mental stress as I recovered from so many things over the span of five years. My body was tired, and I had not done well giving it the care and rest it needed.

Since underlying health issues can contribute to depression, it is wise to see your doctor and rule out any underlying conditions such as thyroid issues, diabetes, or other medical conditions. As I stated at the beginning of this chapter, keep in mind that certain medical conditions can mimic the symptoms of depression, and it will be important to explore these with your doctor before labeling your symptoms only as depression.

Loss

Loss is hard, especially the loss of a loved one, a significant relationship, or even a job. Loss triggers grief, which is an important and healthy process that we need to go through as we navigate losses. We can also experience loss around happy occasions, such as kids graduating and heading to college, moving to a new town, or welcoming a new baby. While there is a lot of excitement around new seasons like these, sometimes we can experience a feeling of loss around a season that has now passed. It's important to grieve the loss of past seasons as much as we are embracing the excitement of the new season in front of us.

It's also important to realize that loss, good or bad, can trigger depression, and we need to stay mindful of the grief process and continue to monitor our progress forward as we navigate this difficult place.

Chemical

Since I am not a certified counselor or a doctor, I will lean on the research and wisdom of others within the mental health field to address the chemical component of depression. This explanation of the role brain chemicals may play in the triggering of depression comes from Harvard Medical School:

"To be sure, chemicals are involved in this process, but it is not a simple matter of one chemical being too low and the other too high. Rather, many chemicals are involved, working both inside and outside nerve cells. There are millions, even billions, of chemical reactions that make up the dynamic system that is responsible for your mood, perceptions, and how you experience life. With this level of complexity, you can see how two people might have similar symptoms of depression, but the problem on the inside, and therefore what treatments will work best, may be entirely different."[v]

From my personal experience, when I visited my doctor, he felt that based on my individual symptoms, I could have a chemical imbalance that was contributing to my overall depression. For that reason, he recommended medication for a specified amount of time to help move me from a state of non-functioning to functioning again. Since we are all uniquely created, I encourage you to seek out the wisdom of a professional counselor and your own doctor as you work on a plan that is best for you and your situation.

Spiritual

Did you know that we are more than just a physical body? It's quite fascinating, in fact.

Every human being has a spiritual nature, regardless of whether they have a religious practice. Since we are physical, as well as spiritual, beings, Christian and non-Christian believers can often unknowingly open the door of their hearts and minds to the work of God's greatest enemy: Satan. This open door allows Satan to enter and wreak havoc on our hearts and minds.

Now, before you think maybe I've watched too many superhero movies, let me share what God's Word says about the spirit realm at work among us.

"For our struggle is not against flesh and blood, but against the rulers, against the authorities, against the powers of this dark world and against the spiritual forces of evil in the heavenly realms." – Ephesians 6:12 (NIV)

This particular passage comes from a letter that Paul wrote while imprisoned in Rome for the first time. It came to the church at Ephesus as a way to encourage the young church. One of Paul's encouragements was for the church to be prepared for battle against the schemes of Satan, who no doubt did not want to see this young church flourish. Just like the Christian believers at Ephesus, we too must be aware of the struggle we face against Satan and his evil forces. His goal is to see us buckle in our battle against depression. I strongly believe this is why God instructs us with these verses in Philippians 4:7-9 (NIV):

> "And the peace of God, which transcends all understanding, will guard your hearts and your minds in Christ Jesus. Finally, brothers and sisters, whatever is true, whatever is noble, whatever is right, whatever is pure, whatever is lovely, whatever is admirable—if anything is praiseworthy—think about such things. Whatever you have learned and received or heard from me, or seen in me—put it into practice. And the God of peace will be with you."

In this passage, God, through Paul, charges the church at Philippi to come to unity after a strong disagreement rose between two women in the church. Apparently, the dispute was big enough to reach Paul, who wrote this impassioned letter to the church of Philippi while imprisoned in Rome.

In his letter, Paul exhorts the church be Christ-focused, to come together in unity, and be mindfully focused on their actions and thoughts.

In the same way, God has given us the clear formula for combating the negative messages and thought patterns that often come with depression and anxiety. We just have to be willing to employ his formula and make it a daily practice in our lives.

While I only listed six possible triggers or causes of depression above, be aware that you could have other triggers that I did not list here. Talking through your possible triggers or causes with your doctor or counselor will be an important conversation to consider having. That type of conversation has the potential to lead to the discovery of therapies or practices best suited to helping you work through your own specific situation and allowing you to better address and manage your depression in the future.

A Word About Suicide

I'll be the first to admit that suicide is not something that most of us want to talk about. It can scare us and make us feel uneasy. If you have ever felt or thought about suicide, it can bring up real feelings of shame and guilt. Yet, I think it's important to understand that suicidal ideation can be a part of depression. Notice I said *can be*, not that it always is. Often, suicidal ideation, passive or active, is a symptom of major depressive disorder and/or bipolar disorder.

By definition, "suicidal ideation means wanting to take your own life or thinking about taking your own life. Passive ideation is when you wish you were dead or that you could die. However, you have no plans or intention of taking your own life. Active ideation, on the other hand, means that you're not only thinking about dying but you are planning how to do it."

It's no secret that suicide continues to be on the rise, in particular among young people. But it also happens among men and women of any age. If you find yourself, either actively or passively, suicidal, I strongly encourage you to call someone who can help you through this dark season, whether it's a counselor, trusted friend, or pastor.

━━━━━━━━━━━━━━━

There is also a 24/7 Suicide Prevention Hotline available for anyone who needs to talk: 1-800-273-TALK (8255)

or

www.suicidepreventionlifeline.org[vii]

━━━━━━━━━━━━━━━

Reaching out to someone is a hard thing to do, but it is the lifeline you need during this time.

I'll be completely vulnerable here and tell you that during the worst of my depression, I found myself passively suicidal. It was one of the hardest things to admit to myself. It was hard to admit that those thoughts were so very present in my mind, yet the pain was so great that often death felt like it might be the only thing that could bring relief.

For a time, I didn't share those thoughts with anyone. Shame marched hard against the door of my heart. Here I was a professing Christian and a pastor's wife with a life that, on the outside, seemed perfect. Admitting those feelings and thoughts scared the daylights out of me and brought a shame down on my shoulders that was hard to bear.

I knew the revelation of those thoughts would hurt those closest to me, in particular, my husband. I vividly remember the first time I spoke to him about it. The hurt and shock on his face was evident. *"But how could you think that was better sweetheart? Why would you purposefully leave me? I need you."*

And I knew he was right.

He did need me. But depression can cloud the mind, making those kinds of realizations almost unrecognizable in the moment.

In my hurting mind, all I could see was the pain I was putting my family through, and I honestly thought they would be better off. Surely my husband could find a better wife and ministry partner, because obviously I was failing miserably at it. Wasn't I?

It took me a long time to realize that death was not better but simply a permanent solution to a temporary problem.

Ultimately, it was the love of my husband and the knowledge that I couldn't ever leave my daughters willingly that brought me back from that place. And I had to believe I would make it through this. I would feel better again, and I would be able to engage in life once more. I had to believe that as I held onto hope, God would not leave me there.

And He didn't leave me there.

Instead, God slowly, in the way only He could, reached into my hurting, dark, and angry heart, and that made all the difference in the world. That was when grace truly stepped into my story.

As we end this chapter, I want to encourage you with this scripture from Psalms 40:1-3 (NLT), a song of King David, as he cried out to the Lord.

"I waited patiently for the Lord to help me, and he turned to me and heard my cry. He lifted me out of the pit of despair, out of the mud and the mire. He set my feet on solid ground and steadied me as I walked along. He has given me a new song to sing, a hymn of praise to our God. Many will see what he has done and be amazed. They will put their trust in the Lord."

That is what I believe for you, my friend—that as you continue to cry out, you will hear and feel the still small voice of God answering you in return and that, in some tangible way, you will begin to see him moving in your life.

Your Turn

1. What signs or symptoms of depression have you noticed in yourself?

2. As you look back, what do you think might have contributed to or triggered your depression?

3. Have you taken the time to see a qualified professional counselor or doctor? If not, what might be holding you back?

4. Do you struggle with suicidal ideation? If so, who can you talk to that feels safe and can help you during this difficult season?

This Week's Activity

Take time this week to pray and ask God to show you what may have contributed or led to your depression. Was there a significant life event? Can you see a hereditary trait or any other factors? Sometimes being able to identify a trigger or starting point can be helpful in the healing process. Write down what you discover or sense. This may be helpful information to share with your doctor or counselor as you are in their care.

"Save me, O God, for the waters have come up to my neck.
I sink in the miry depths, where there is no foothold.
I have come into the deep waters; the floods engulf me.
I am worn out calling for help; my throat is parched.
My eyes fail, looking for my God."
PSALM 69: 1-3 (NIV)

CHAPTER 3

God's Word and Depression

I have to admit that at the beginning of my depression journey, I didn't really know what God had to say about depression or anxiety. It's not that I hadn't been a student of the Bible. In fact, I was raised in the church, attended my fair share of Sunday School, and sat through many a sermon. As a ministry leader, I had spent countless years studying the Bible as I readied for retreats and leading small group studies. So it wasn't that I didn't know the Bible, it's just that I never gave a whole lot of thought to what the Bible had to say about depression. When you don't struggle in a particular area, rarely do you go looking for answers. That is, until you're knee-deep in questions.

Over the years, when I would sit and listen to other women share their struggles with depression or anxiety, I often went to Scripture as a way to offer hope and encouragement, which was entirely appropriate and most certainly heartfelt on my end. However, having now been on the other end, I hope that during those meetings I was encouraging and didn't just hand out Scripture like it was candy or a band-aid for their hearts.

Often, that can be our tendency as believers. We hand out Scripture without thinking about context or extending empathy for the heart of the person to whom we're trying to bring comfort. Often our heart has the purest of intentions, but sometimes our actions can still cause a wound if we are not careful to heed the heart of those we are sharing with.

Let me just say, too, that if you are someone who has been handed Scripture as a band-aid, in the hopes that it would fix your depression, I am deeply sorry. God's Word was never meant to be a band-aid for your heart. So what exactly is the purpose of God's Word then? To quote Charles Stanley:

> "[God's Word, the Bible,] is the unfolding revelation of almighty God. From beginning to end, the Lord demonstrates His love and concern for His people. He gives us amazing promises and has the infinite power to fulfill them. Help for every circumstance of life is found within the Scriptures."[viii]

In the Bible, we find more than simply help. First and foremost, we find salvation from the sin that weighs us down and, secondly, we find the revelation of the nature and character of Christ–the very nature that in seasons of hardship will give us strength, hope, wisdom, and guidance to continue fighting forward.

Not only that, but we also find story after story of the giants of the Christian faith who struggled with deep sorrow, turmoil, devastation, heartbreak, and downcast spirits. Did you catch that? Giants of the faith. Giants of the faith who struggled like you and me because while they were ruling countries, preaching the gospel, and leading people, they were also deeply human. They experienced and felt all the joy, pain, and sorrow of this world just as we do now.

The Power and Importance of God's Word in Fighting Depression

So why would I start with God's Word? Wouldn't it make more sense to first talk about doctors, counselors, and all the other ways we battle depression? Maybe. But in my experience, I have found that starting with God's Word has a direct correlation to moving with strength from the darkness of depression to the light. Just like a house must have a foundation laid before the walls can go up, so we must lay a foundation for starting this depression battle.

Have you ever seen a house with a poor foundation? It's not a pretty sight. Having worked alongside my husband in construction for many years, I've seen what happens when you have a poor foundation. Initially, the house may look great, but when you start seeing significant cracks in the ceiling, on the exterior of the house, or along the chimney, you know you've got a problem. That is why, as I lay out the framework of how I walked out of the darkness of depression, I start with God's Word. It is truly the underpinning—the foundation—that holds everything else in my life together even when the world falls apart.

Through all my years growing up, attending Sunday School and chapel services at my Christian high school, I heard frequent teachings and sermons about the power of God's Word. I honestly didn't have trouble believing in the power of God's Word from a knowledge standpoint, but it would take the fire of depression to finally drive home this truth at a deeper heart level.

It wasn't until I finally got Scripture out of my head and into my heart, through implementing a daily practice of writing down Scripture, reciting it to myself, and posting it where I would see it, that I truly felt and saw the power of God's Word released in my life in practical and tangible ways.

So let's take a look at a few things in God's Word. In all honesty, most people might start by sharing all the great verses about God's love and his grace and mercy, and, most assuredly, those are powerful and comforting verses. There have been many days, even now, when those very verses reach deep into the places that still hurt or bring comfort for situations that can still be hard. And we will look at those verses, but first I want to share a verse with you that often can be tough to hear. Yet, it is one that I have found has brought a lot of perspective in this battle. It is found in Hebrews, where the writers of this book are exhorting the persecuted Jewish believers to continue to mature and persevere in their faith.

> "For the word of God is living and active, sharper than any two-edged sword, piercing to the division of soul and of spirit, of joints and of marrow, and discerning the thoughts and intentions of the heart." – Hebrews 4:12 (ESV)

I'll admit that some of the verses in the Bible are easier to receive than others. During my battle with depression, I often wrestled with God's love for me. If He really loved me, why wouldn't He just reach down and make it all better? Zap me and make all the pain go away and make my world right again? Why did I have to work through the pain, suffer the loss of relationship, and relearn to live in a world that felt so changed? And while I firmly believe God has the power to reach out and heal us immediately, I realize that, for most of us, it will be a journey. It is in this journey that God allows us (notice I didn't say "causes us") to go through a refining of our hearts and souls.

I used to see Hebrews 4:12 as a harsh taskmaster—a verse that only applied when I sinned and needed correction.

However, somewhere in this fight with depression, I realized that sometimes God graciously uses his Word to cut to the heart of my pain, to expose the places of hurt so that, ultimately, I could heal. Never did he push his way through. He always waited until I came to him and asked. He's a gentleman like that. Honestly, the best way I can describe His patience is that it's like an onion that you peel layer by layer until you get down to its core. That's how God works to reach our hearts. He peels back the layers as we're ready to get to the heart of who He's truly created us to be. But that peeling part is not always fun. It can feel much like a surgery, and healing from that kind of heart surgery takes time.

I also liken it to an experience I had a few years ago. When I was in my thirties, I had to have major sinus surgery. For years, I had ongoing migraines, along with frequent sinus infections that often turned into bronchitis several times a year. As I searched for relief from the pain and frustrating yearly sickness, my doctor recommended that I see an ENT specialist. After some testing, the ENT came into the exam room and declared, *"Well, I've got good news and bad news."*

Steeling myself for the worst, I waited for his next words.

"The good news is that your septum (the bone inside your nose that keeps it straight) can't get any more deviated than it already is. It's literally touching the opposite side of your nose

and causing issues with your breathing and sinus function. Plus, you seem to be missing sinus cavities in your frontal lobe, which is probably the reason for all the pressure and pain in your head."

If that was the good news, I hated to hear what the bad news was.

He continued, *"The bad news is that in order to fix it and to give you relief, we will need to do a pretty extensive sinus surgery. It's entirely up to you, but if you want relief, it's what I would recommend."*

I won't bore you or gross you out with all the details, but, in the end, I decided that the pain and recovery from surgery would be worth the relief and healing it would bring after years of pain and misery. While I would never want to go through that surgery again, I am so glad that I chose temporary pain for the benefit of no longer experiencing migraines or sinus issues. I still get sick from time to time, but the frequency is nothing compared to the years before that surgery.

In the same way, for those of us dealing with depression, we have to decide if it's worth addressing the pain and allowing God to dig deep in our hearts and minds so that he can begin to bring healing where it is needed most. It means allowing him to start peeling back the layers of pain, wounds, and dark places so that, ultimately, we can heal.

But this is not just about how God wants to do surgery on our hearts; it's also about how he carries us in this battle towards healing, if we let him. Pay careful attention to the part where we are asked to take action and the results we will experience if we follow and apply God's Word to our lives.

> "Your word is a lamp to guide my feet and a light for my path." – Psalm 119:105 (NLT)

> "My son, pay attention to what I say; turn your ears to my words. Do not let them out of your sight, keep them within your heart; for they are life to those who find them and health to one's whole body. Above all else, guard your heart, for everything you do flows from it." – Proverbs 4:20-23 (NIV)

Did you catch that? His Word is a lamp. A big ole flashlight. The very thing that will shed light on our next step. Sometimes in the darkness of depression we don't know what step to take next. When I was lying on that couch, I couldn't see the way out. In fact, I wasn't even looking for the next step because I wanted the whole picture. I wanted the assurance that everything was going to be okay. I wanted to know that *if* I decided to start walking, it would all turn out fine. But life doesn't give us those kinds of assurances. As far as I know, no one has ever been able to see their whole life laid out before them before they start living it.

In that moment, the moment I made a choice to get up from the couch, I also had to become okay with just taking the next best step without knowing the full outcome. That day, all I knew to do was walk around the cow field. The next day, I did the same thing again. I had no guarantee my life would get better—but I had to try. I was tired of not living.

But get this. Not only did I have to decide to start walking, but, as Psalm 119:105 says above, I had to be willing to carry the lamp of God's Word on my journey. During those years that we lived in that beautiful mountain town, we had to learn to keep oil lamps on hand for when the power went out. And the power went out frequently, sometimes even on a sunny day. If a tree went down from a storm and took out a transformer line, hundreds of people would be without power until they could get it fixed. So we had oil lamps. Yes, the old-fashioned kind where you trim the wick, add oil to the base, and then, once lighted, place the glass globe back on the lamp.

Now imagine with me that we had a storm and the lights went out at night. No worries, we have an oil lamp. Let's say I light that oil lamp and set it on the table so we can see. Well, that lamp is great and keeps us from tripping over stuff...as long as we're in the same room. But, what if we decide to go to the next room and leave the light sitting on the table? All of the sudden, the light is of no use because we left it sitting on the table.

God's Word is the same way.

It is a light for our lives, but if we refuse to meditate on it, learn from it, be changed by it, let it guide us (light our path), we're no better able to find our way than when we left the lamp on our dining room table. How can God quicken something to our hearts if we refuse to even take it in? If I want to be able to discern my next steps, I have got to carry God's Word with me every day, no matter the season or storm. My trust must be in God and his Word during this battle, not in what I can figure out on my own.

I've heard it said that our level of peace is in direct proportion to the object of our trust. When I heard that, it shook me. Where was the object of my trust for this battle? Was it in myself? Was it being placed in others? Or was I placing my trust in the only One who could truly bring peace and carry me through this battle?

I'll be honest, there are still days I struggle to trust God fully. My human nature, like yours, begs for something more tangible than what faith feels like or what trust looks like. We want to be able to hold those promises in our hands like we hold a beautiful flower just picked from the garden. Yet, what God asks of us is to trust him—even when we can't see. And honestly, that might be the hardest battle of them all.

Even Kings Are Shaken

Every time I lead a depression support group or counsel other women, I hear this comment over and over again: *"When I was at my last church, someone told me that if I struggled with depression it was because my faith wasn't strong enough and I just needed to pray more."*

And as I sit across from those women, my heart cringes. It sees the hurt, pain, and sometimes anger that play across their faces as they stare back at me through tear-filled eyes. The words spoken from the lips of well-intentioned people have done their work; they have cut deep into their hearts, but never in the way God intended. While depression and anxiety test our faith, very rarely is it because of a lack of faith. Depression is much more complex than that, not to mention that the phrase "have more faith" is such an ambiguous one. What does "have more faith" even mean?

In Chapter 5, we will talk more about the role of faith in our depression battle and explore practical ways that we can strengthen and bolster our faith. However, for now, let's take a look at some of the giants of faith who also faced depression and anxiety.

King David

It was during the most painful parts of my journey that I found solace and relief in the Psalms, where many of David's songs and laments (prayers of sorrow) are found. My heart resonated with the thoughts and feelings of King

David and his deepest moments of devastation and sorrow. God called David a man after His own heart. David was also king over all of Israel, yet he struggled greatly when his own people turned against him and he found himself chased by men who wanted him dead. In Psalms 42:5 (NIV) we read what many Bible scholars believe is a lament of David that he presented to the Sons of Korah (a group of Levites, serving as gatekeepers for the temple):

"Why, my soul, are you downcast? Why so disturbed within me? Put your hope in God, for I will yet praise Him, my Savior and my God."

And we know from further reading of the Scripture that each time David cried out, God was always faithful to him in that moment of need. David would become one of the greatest kings of Israel's history; yet, I can imagine in the time of his greatest sorrow, he wasn't always sure that would be true. It's got to be hard to believe that you'll be a great king when people are chasing you because they want to kill you. Sure, we know the whole picture now, but King David didn't. But he found solace and a deep, abiding trust in the God who rescued him despite his sin, despite his lies and deceit, and despite his humanness. God kept showing up, just like he does for you and me.

Job

During the darkest parts of my depression, my heart also resonated with the story of Job in a deep way—in such a deep way that I don't know if I can really describe it adequately. I remember reading the whole book with new eyes and, for the first time in my Christian walk, beginning to have an inkling of what Job suffered. His pain often seemed to mimic my own inner pain, with his questions echoing in the chambers of my own heart.

If you aren't familiar with the story, Job was a rich and godly man, with lots of material wealth, children, houses, and animals. He was also well-respected in his town and served the Lord with a pure heart. In fact, Scripture tells us that God said this of Job in Job 1:8 (ESV) "Then the Lord said to Satan, 'Have you considered my servant Job, that there is none like him on the earth, a blameless and upright man, who fears God and turns away from evil?" Job was doing everything right in the Lord's eyes until the day Satan wanted to test him, convinced Job would fall away from God if everything were taken from him. And God allowed the testing. As Job's worldly possessions, children, servants, and animals are striped away, we read of Job's descent into grief and deep sorrow.

"Why did I not perish at birth, and die as I came from the womb?" Job 3:11(NIV)

"I have no peace, no quietness, I have no rest, but only turmoil." Job 3:26 (NIV)

"I loathe my very life, therefore I will give free rein to my complaint and speak out in the bitterness of my soul." Job 10:1 (NIV)

After all that loss, who wouldn't feel depressed? When we lost everything because of the bankruptcy our business suffered, I felt a little like Job. Gone were all the things we had worked so hard for; gone were our relationships; gone was our means to feed our family and provide clothes for our children. Gone. Utterly gone. How many days did I feel like Job, wanting to curl up in a hole and die? How many days did I wonder where God was? Had He abandoned us, even though we were faithfully serving his people in ministry? There was so much that didn't make sense in those days, but I took comfort in knowing that, despite all of Job's trials, God still rescued him in the end. Because of that, I still had hope—as small as it might have been.

Jonah

While Jonah was a man after God's own heart as well, he also decided that running away from God was a good idea. (Hint: It's really not. Where are you going to go that he can't see you?) But even Jonah finally came around to obeying. However, after spending three days and nights in the belly of the whale, Jonah *still* struggled with God's decision to save the city of Nineveh. Jonah thought God should destroy it and, when God said "no," Jonah became so angry and depressed that he began to despise his own life.

> "Now Lord, take away my life, for it is better for me to die than to live." Jonah 4:3 (NIV)

That's some pretty intense sorrow right there. Can you relate? I know there were times I felt a similar way, and maybe you have too. The point I am trying to make is that sorrow, depression, grief, loss, fear, and being overwhelmed are not new to the human condition. And they most certainly are not new to God's people and Christian believers today.

In this chapter, I only listed three of the more prominent characters in the Bible who struggled with deep despair, but as you spend time reading God's Word, you will see that many others struggled as well. The one common denominator between all of these characters is that they cried out to God, and then waited, sometimes longer than I'm sure they wished to.

I know there were days in my journey when I wasn't sure if God heard me at all. Sometimes, it felt like I was shouting at the ceiling only to hear my own voice bounce back down to my hurting heart. Yet, I kept crying out. I kept seeking. And it was in that seeking that God began to break through for me. As it says in Psalm 91:15 (NIV):

"He will call on me, and I will answer him; I will be with him in trouble, I will deliver him and honor him."

And again in Jeremiah 29:12-13 (NIV):

"Then you will call upon Me and come and pray to Me, and I will listen to you. You will seek Me and find Me when you search for Me with all your heart."

The important part to remember and note is that God *did* answer. In the same way, as you and I cry out to God in our own hurt, confusion, and despair, he hears us too. He may not always answer in the way that we expect him to, or as quickly as we want him to, but the point is, He does answer if we just watch for it. He may show up through other people, through a podcast you're listening to, or a song that plays on the radio. In my own journey, as I started attuning my heart to God's Word and asking God to show up for me, I began to see the small ways that he was there: providing a doctor's appointment right when I needed it, my late-night Google search for a counselor that resulted in me finding Lynn, the counselor that would journey through the hard places with me, and the moments He helped calm my panic in large crowds.

Even if you're having a hard time believing it right now, I just want to remind you that He sees you. He sees you and loves you in the very place you find yourself, and just as He did not abandon the great men of the Bible, just as He did not abandon me, He will not abandon you either. If you need to, borrow my hope for a little while until your eyes begin to see how He is showing up for you in this battle forward.

Your Turn

1. When you hear Scripture, is it hard for you to receive? If so, why do you think that is?

2. What wounds are you still carrying from well-meaning people? Are you willing to forgive so that you can move forward?

3. Which Bible character do you most identify with and why?

4. Are you carrying the Word of God with you, just like the oil lamp illustration, or is it sitting on the table?

This Week's Activity

Write down at least three verses that encourage you on sticky notes or index cards. Place the verses where you can see them every day—on a mirror, in your car, or in your day planner—and commit to reading them each day. As a further challenge, work to memorize at least two of those verses and commit them to memory. The goal is to start hiding God's Word in your heart so that you can carry God's Word wherever you go. You will be amazed at how, as you begin to memorize Scripture, those verses will come to mind to serve you in your moments of need.

*"The Truth is: Belonging starts with self-acceptance.
Your level of belonging, in fact, can never be greater
than your level of self-acceptance,
because believing that you're enough
is what gives you the courage to be
authentic, vulnerable and imperfect."*

— BRENÉ BROWN

CHAPTER 4

When Others Fail Us

It was during the deepest part of my depression that I had this thought: *"Maybe, just maybe, I'm simply too broken to be loved. Is that possible?"* I thought to myself, *"It must be."* That had to explain it. The silence. This life that used to be filled with coffee dates and invites to dinner and phone calls to say hello or talk just because.

Other than one lone friend who sent me an occasional text message to see how I was, my world fell quiet. The phone stopped ringing. My message inbox sat devastatingly empty, and my email no longer chimed with incoming messages. The silence was both deafening and defining. There was so much of the silence I didn't understand. Where had everyone gone?

Up until my struggle with depression, I would have said with 100 percent certainty that I had people in my life who would stick with me through thick and thin. People, who when a crisis arose, would gather around me and my family, offering love and support through the tough season. They had done it before when our children were born, through the years when I had to have multiple surgeries, and when my husband was confined to bed as he waited for back surgery. They showed up with meals, cards, and messages that spoke of their love and care for us as a family. There was nothing to indicate they wouldn't do that again.

But that's not my story. Instead, when the darkest storm came, the majority of people departed from our lives. And it hurt. Deeply. Abandonment creates a deep soul wound that is hard to heal. It brings its own sort of devastation to our minds and hearts.

It was that abandonment during those silent days that led me to the conclusion that I was simply too broken to be loved. I must be, right? That's why everyone had left, right? My brokenness was too much to handle. And while it made me sad and angry, I didn't blame them. As I looked over the landscape of my life, all I could see were the places I had failed myself and the places I had let down those I had been tasked to serve. I would have abandoned myself if I could. In the fog of my pain, I determined that this level of failure and brokenness deserved abandonment. In fact, I wouldn't have blamed God if He wanted to walk away too.

On this side of that journey, I realize that the hearts and intentions of the people in my life were not to make me feel abandoned or leave us on our own to navigate this painful season. Some of them simply did not know what to do or how to help.

From my experience, the normal human flesh response, in particular when someone is struggling through depression or anxiety, is to pull back, thinking that what the person struggling needs the most is space and time to heal. I think it would be easier if depression came with a cast or crutches or something visible for people to see. Depression feels so confusing, complicated, and, at times, scary for people that the only thing they know to do is pull away.

I remember standing with a friend one time, visiting on her front porch, and she leaned in and said, *"Victoria, I have this friend. She's really struggling with depression. I want to help her but I don't know what to do. I figure I should just give her space. Doesn't she need quiet and space to heal, to hear from God or something?"*

While I understood my friend's heart, I immediately responded, *"No, don't pull away; instead, I challenge you to lean in. I know it won't be easy or comfortable, but what she needs most right now is the presence of people. You don't have to say anything or fix anything; just be present. Send her a card, call her on the phone, stop by and see her. She doesn't need grand gestures, just simple reminders that you are still there."*

Presence is a funny thing. It requires sitting, not having to say anything, and that can be hard for us to do when we so desperately want to help those we love. Desperation to help can lead some people to go a bit overboard. Instead of pulling away, it feels like they continually approach you with Bible verse after Bible verse and prayer after prayer, just hoping something will stick. That something will fix whatever is broken. They may say things like: *"This verse really helped me and I know if you just believe it enough, it will work for you."* Or they may say: *"Just have more faith. Your faith is not strong enough. Just have more faith."* Their desperation to help drives them to wound, and, most of the time, they don't even know they are doing it.

And while Scripture is powerful, as we talked about in Chapter 3, it needs to be given in a life-giving way, not as a band-aid fix to our thoughts and emotions. The reality is that those struggling through depression need the presence of people most. Isolation from others only makes depression worse. It often compounds the sense of hopelessness and adds to the loneliness that many feel. For me, it was that one friend and her random text messages that became my lifeline to the outside world. To this day, I am grateful for that thread of hope woven through my story. Because of her, a small flame of hope and faith dared to flicker in the dark.

The hard truth is that we may never know all the reasons why someone walks out of our lives during our struggle with depression, or why they withdraw to a safe distance or even vanish entirely. We can really struggle when people walk away and disappear. The emotions and feelings around that abandonment are real and deeply painful. Yet, and this is the truth I have come to realize for myself, for whatever reason, not everyone is going to be able to walk with you on this journey. Not everyone is going to be able to handle the pain, the emotion, and the change that comes with things like depression and anxiety. Often we think it's because we're just unlovable, or we're not worth the time of friendship, when the truth is, there may be things in their life that keep them from drawing close. Whatever the reason for their vanishing, if we are going to move forward, we have to be willing to forgive and let them go.

So how do we push past the feelings of abandonment, loneliness, fear, and anger that want to take over when someone walks away? Here are some reminders and practical tips to help you start navigating those painful waters. These are the things that helped me move past the loneliest points of my journey and that I still do to this day when loneliness wants to rear its ugly head.

How to Keep Walking Even When You Feel Alone

✦ Understand that what you are feeling is valid. When others fail us, it does make us feel abandoned, forgotten, angry, hopeless, and lonely. These emotions are ones we need to work through in a healthy way before they turn into ongoing bitterness and resentment.

✦ Extend forgiveness to those who could not walk with you in this season. You may never fully know the reason why they couldn't, but extending forgiveness to them is what will ultimately allow your heart to start healing.

✦ Look for places to stay connected to healthy people and community. I know this is a hard one. I will never tell you that this part is easy. Because of depression and what is happening inside our bodies, we have to fight the urge to withdraw into ourselves. It may feel safer to withdraw, but withdrawing can make depression worse, especially if there is no one there to help counter the negative thinking and emotions that often kick into overdrive when we keep to ourselves.

✦ Pray and ask God to send one or two friends who can walk with you in this season. I remember asking God this, and while I wasn't really sure He would answer, He sent me a counselor. A literal counselor. For two years, I had kept things bottled up because I didn't know who to trust. The anger was so deep that I wasn't sure if anyone would be willing to handle it and help me work through it. Then God sent me Lynn and, through her guidance and compassion, God began to bring healing and relief from the deep inner pain I felt.

None of the steps above are easy. I get that. So many things feel hard when you're battling depression. Getting up, going to work, engaging in simple conversation, processing information, eating, getting dressed, etc., all feels like such a huge mountain to overcome. It's going to take willingness and intentionality to keep stepping forward, regardless of whether anyone comes along with you.

Your Worth and a 20-dollar Bill

During one of the first depression support groups I led, I shared an illustration I had seen a number of different times over the years from various pastors and speakers. Every time it is a powerful reminder of my own value and worth in God's eyes, and I wanted a visual way of sharing that with my group.

Standing in front of my group, I pulled out a crisp, 20-dollar bill. I showed it around the circle and asked, *"How much is this worth?"* They each answered accordingly, *"20 dollars."* I then proceeded to drop it on the floor and step on it. Picking up my foot and rescuing the 20 dollars from the floor, I asked them again, *"How much is it worth now?"* Again, they replied, *"20 dollars."* This time, I took the 20-dollar bill in my hand, crumbled it, and rubbed it between my fingers until it was wrinkled and out of shape. As I uncurled it, I held it up. *"How much now?"* With a slight smile on their faces, they responded, *"20 dollars."* One last time, I took the 20-dollar bill, wrinkled and crumpled, and dropped it on the ground. Raising my boot-clad foot, I stomped all over it, rubbing it into the floor. Finally, I picked it up and said, *"Okay, how much is it worth now?"* With heads nodding and a few tears, they replied, *"20 dollars."*

I paused before saying, *"Exactly. The worth of this bill did not diminish based on what has been done to it, no matter how dirty or crumpled or wrinkled it became. At the end of the day, it is still worth 20 dollars. Its value never changed. The bank will still deposit it, and you can still spend it at the store. It has the same worth now as the day it was printed."*

The same is true of you and me. No matter what has happened to us in this life, no matter what has been done to us or where we have failed, our worth in God's eyes never, ever changes. Yet, when you are battling depression, your worth is one of the key areas that Satan works to defeat you in. If he can get us believing that we have no worth, depression becomes our bondage—not just a piece of our bigger story. Psalms 139:13-16 (NIV) says this about us:

> "For you created my innermost being; you knit me together in my mother's womb. I praise you because I am fearfully and wonderfully made; your works are wonderful, I know that full well. My frame was not hidden from you when I was made in the secret place, when I was woven together in the depths of the earth. Your eyes saw my unformed body; all the days ordained

for me were written in your book before one of them came to be."

I understand that embracing our worth is hard to do. It has been incredibly hard for me to do too. We are so intimately aware of our own shortcomings that we don't even love ourselves. And when you add the pain of losing people in our lives to this thing called depression we, understandably, question our worth.

But I share this hope with you: Even if everyone else walks away, there is One who stays close and, overwhelmingly, still calls us His. Isaiah 43:1 (NIV) says:

"But now, this is what the Lord says...'Do not fear, for I have redeemed you; I have summoned you by name, you are mine.'"

Did you catch that? We are His. We can't get away from that truth, whether we believe it or not. That truth and His Word stand, and so do the things He says about us. So how do we start believing those things and find healing for our wounded hearts and minds?

At some point in my depression journey, I realized that I needed to start identifying the lies that I believed about my worth, my brokenness, and myself. I needed to trade in the lies for truth. If I ever wanted to gain victory over my depression, I was going to have to fight for it.

It was going to take grit, grace, and faith to get through the lies, to identify the enemy (Hint: It wasn't the people around me) and refuse to be duped anymore. I needed to start believing the truth of God's Word over my own feelings, and that honestly scared me. It meant I had to take responsibility and own my own stuff. I had stop pointing fingers and shifting blame, despite what others may have done to add to the weight of my depression. It was time to take back what the enemy was determined to steal.

Believing in My Worth Again

Did you know that there is someone out there whose sole job it is to destroy us? No, I'm not talking about the difficult neighbor next door or the coworker who acts like Meryl Streep in *The Devil Wears Prada*. While we all have to deal with difficult people, the "someone" I am talking about is Satan. 1 Peter 5:8 (NLT) says:

> "Stay alert! Watch out for your great enemy, the devil. He prowls around like a roaring lion looking for someone to devour."

Ephesians 6:12 (NIV) also warns us:

> "For our struggle is not against flesh and blood, but against the rulers, against the authorities, against the

powers of this dark world and against the spiritual forces of evil in the heavenly realms."

Both of these Bible verses make us aware that our fight is not ultimately against the people in our lives. When we are battling depression, the mind is already under attack, making us even more susceptible to the enemy. And one of the key places that Satan determines to attack us is through our thoughts. He brings thoughts of doubt about our worth and inadequacy, along with feelings of shame and overwhelm. He knows that if he can win the battle for our minds, we become ineffective for God's kingdom and possibly even turn away from our Creator. Everything about him is deceptive; there is no good in him.

And he is a hard enemy to face. During the worst of my depression, as I struggled with feelings of abandonment and questioned my worth, Satan was leading the charge, tempting me to believe that I was too broken to be loved. The Bible says that Satan can disguise himself as an angel of light. The lies he told me were subtle and whispered and sometimes held just enough truth to make them believable. In 2 Corinthians 11:14 (NIV), we read:

"And no wonder, for Satan himself masquerades as an angel of light."

This is where knowing, understanding, and hiding God's Word in our heart is so very important. Remember when we talked about Hebrews 4:12 in Chapter 3? That verse starts out by reminding us that God's Word is sharper than any two-edged sword. His Word is what will reveal the truth and allow us to test the things we are hearing, seeing, and believing in our lives.

And we need to test these things because, as an angel of light, Satan is very good at adding just enough truth to make a lie believable: *"They walked away from you. See, it's because you are too broken to be loved,"* he would whisper. *"If they really loved you, they wouldn't have left,"* he would taunt.

It would be three years into my battle with depression before I had the chance to test that lie and find the courage to ask past friends if it was true. As I sat with them that day, I hesitantly asked, *"Was I too broken to be loved? Was that it? Was that why you had to walk away from me?"* They assured me it wasn't true, and they told me that they made the choice to step back because of the deep anger they saw in me. They felt that they needed some boundaries for themselves, and they made the choice to step back, giving me space to find healing.

Those words were hard for me to hear because, at the beginning of my depression, I had no idea I was so angry. It wasn't until I spent time in counseling that I began to see how the anger had built up in my life and was affecting the relationships around me. Remember in Chapter 2 when we were reviewing the signs and symptoms of depression? Deep internal anger is one of those signs that I missed for a long time. And while it made me sad that they felt they had to walk away, it helped me realize that I believed a lie. I wasn't too broken to be loved; they just couldn't walk with me in that season because of what was happening in their own lives and what they felt they needed in that moment.

This is where grace must come in—grace for yourself and grace for others. The giving and receiving of that grace is what allowed me to start, ever so slowly, believing that I did have worth. And while believing in my own worth started with grace, it also led me to understand that I must choose who I listen to. When you fight depression, you also fight the voices in your head continually whispering that you're not good enough to be loved.

Defeating those voices starts with being aware of and acknowledging the lies. Whatever we allow ourselves to be influenced by will always be the leading voice in the symphony of our lives. So how did I overcome the spinning, negative, and emotion-driven unhealthy thoughts? Here are four key practices I began to implement into my life on a daily basis that allowed me to step out of the chaos of my own mind.

1. I had to take every thought captive.
     ◇ I would often write down encouraging Scripture and post it on my bathroom mirror, in my car, and

inside my computer. I spent time memorizing scripture and hiding it deep in my heart.

✧ Proverbs 4:23(NIV) says: "Above all else, guard your heart, for everything you do flows from it." What are you allowing to hide in your heart?

2. I had to be careful of what I was reading, watching, and listening to.

✧ The world is not on our side. It feeds everyone a steady stream of music, shows, and news that is anything but life-giving. I started to keep a close eye on what I was allowing myself to watch and listen to. As much as I love country music, songs about breaking up, getting revenge, or partying 'till the cows come home was not exactly uplifting. However, when I spent time listening to worship music, my thoughts began to naturally turn and my mood lifted. What we listen to and watch matters, whether we like to admit it or not.

3. I had to resist shame.

✧ Understanding the difference between shame and guilt was key in helping me let go of the feelings of unworthiness. Brené Brown, a shame researcher, explains the difference like this: Shame says that there is something wrong with me; with how I was created in my deepest self. Guilt, on the other hand, says I simply did something wrong.[ix]

This is what Brené Brown goes on to say about the power of shame:

> "When we experience shame, we feel disconnected and desperate for worthiness. Full of shame or the fear of shame, we are more likely to engage in self-destructive behaviors and to attack or shame others. In fact, shame is related to violence, aggression, depression, addiction, eating disorders, and bullying."[x]

Resisting shame was hard but vital to helping me win my battle with depression and truly embracing who God had created me to be.

4. I had to make a conscious choice to believe what God said about me, namely that He loved me, and that I still had worth to Him and those around me.

   ✧ While my feelings (and your feelings) are valid, I came to realize that my feelings can't always be trusted. I had to make a conscious choice every day to believe God over my feelings. It took time, but after practicing this choice daily, the ongoing thoughts of self-hatred, loathing, anger, hopelessness, and loneliness began to be replaced with God's peace, love for myself, hope, and less frequent moments of loneliness. It was gradual, but that daily choice made all the difference in the world.

At the end of the day, we don't have the ability to make people stay. There will be those who, for whatever reason, are not able to walk with you through the painful season of depression. Letting go of the expectation that people will stay or can fix things will be key for allowing your heart to heal. Letting go will give you the ability to take the next steps in your journey, which includes taking practical steps towards wholeness.

Your Turn

1. Have you experienced others failing you when you felt you needed them most? How have you dealt with this?

2. How have you allowed what others may have done or said to affect you? How might that be negatively impacting your depression journey?

3. What lies do you think you may believe about your worth, how others see you, or how God sees you? Once you identify the lie(s), take time to write out the counteracting truth(s).

4. What stood out to you about this week's reading? How might you apply it to your life this week?

This Week's Activity

Take some time this week to identify whether there is a wound of abandonment in your life. Acknowledge it, pray through it, and give it to God. You may even need to spend some time processing this with a counselor or pastor. Also identify one person who has been there for you, even in a small way. For me, it was the friend who would text me occasionally to see how I was doing. Send a note of thanks to that friend, expressing your gratitude for their support.

*"Authenticity is a collection of choices
that we have to make every day.
It's about the choice to show up and be real.
The choice to be honest.
The choice to let our true selves be seen."*

— Brené Brown

CHAPTER 5

Practical Steps to Wholeness

One of the things I struggled with when it came to my depression was knowing what practical steps I could take to move forward and find relief and healing. I did a ton of research, scoured resources, and sought advice from others.

While I found a few helpful suggestions, I had a hard time finding anything concrete to help me develop a practical, day-to-day plan. Too often, we make the mistake of thinking that just one thing, like medicine or counseling, will completely fix our depression. When it doesn't, we get discouraged. The reality is that depression is complex and it's important that we tackle it from several different angles. It took some work, but, over time, I was able to develop a holistic plan that worked for me and addressed my depression from various angles.

That is why I'll be spending some time in this chapter talking about some of the practical steps I took to address my depression. It was important that I not only tackled my depression and anxiety with a number of different approaches but also, once those approaches were identified, set a plan in place to make them happen daily.

Keep in mind that one size does not fit all when it comes to a plan. What worked for me may not work for you. You may need to explore different ways to address additional areas of concern. However, I do hope that reading through some of these steps will help get you started towards making a holistic plan for your own journey forward.

Medical

One of the first practical steps I took was making an appointment to see my doctor. I can't say I reached that point easily though. Early on, my husband begged me to go see our family doctor, but I was hesitant. You remember in Chapter 4, when I talked about shame? Well, shame was rearing its ugly head trying to convince me that seeing my doctor was a waste of time and that he probably would just think I was making things up.

Finally, at the gentle insistence of my husband, I agreed to make an appointment. I was confident I wouldn't be able to get in for weeks because my doctor was usually busy with other patients. However, the morning we called, there had just been a cancellation, and I was able to be seen that afternoon. That in itself felt like a miracle to me and, in some small way, I felt that maybe God did see me and cared enough to clear the way. My fragile bit of hope was gently fanned into a flickering flame by that one phone call.

And while that conversation with my doctor was not easy, I gathered my little bit of courage and began to share how I was feeling. After doing a brief exam and asking some gentle but pointed questions, he recommended a depression medication that he felt would help me move from a state of despair to being able to function once again.

I will always be thankful for his care and how he helped me put a plan in place for taking medication that I wouldn't have to be on forever. I wanted a plan to come off of the medication eventually. Together, we decided that I would stay on the medication for one year. We would evaluate at that point and discontinue it if I was doing well. There was no guarantee that one year would be long enough, but I was willing to take one small step at a time knowing that my doctor would work with me to arrive at the best care plan for me.

Thankfully, I was able to come off the medication within that year. The medication, while it did not lift the grayness from my world, helped me get off the couch and begin to function again. I was able to go out, do things with my family, and be present for my children.

Your care plan may look different, with different types of medications or therapies. Whatever that plan looks like,

I encourage you to continue advocating for your health by working hand in hand with your doctor and not allowing shame to keep you from seeking help.

Shame, as I said earlier, will want to rear its ugly head, trying to convince you that seeing a doctor is somehow weak or shows a lack of faith on your part. Let me be clear that going to your doctor and taking medication for your depression or anxiety is not weakness or a lack of faith in God's ability to heal you. I realize that there may be people in your life who tell you those things. However, as hard as it is, we need to let those comments roll off our backs and keep fighting for our mental health. While their opinion may be shared with concern, the reality is that this is your life, and you are the one who gets the final say in how you are going to fight your depression.

I truly believe that God sometimes chooses to use the very doctors or psychiatrists He has gifted to help us in these circumstances. I was fortunate to have a doctor who had known me since I was in high school. He knew the day I came into his office that something was not right. He never questioned whether I was telling the truth or making anything up. However, I know that is not everyone's story. Maybe you have tried to go to the doctor or psychiatrist and you don't feel heard or seen. I encourage you to continue advocating for your health and find a doctor who will listen. I know it can be tedious and tiring to find the right doctor, but it will be worth having this important advocate on your side.

Professional Counseling

It actually took me two years to finally see a professional counselor following my initial visit to my primary care doctor. It wasn't because I didn't know or understand the value of counseling. I simply did not know who to trust, much less who to see.

I knew I wanted to meet with a Christ-centered counselor, but I was afraid of getting someone weird. Seriously, that was my biggest fear. All I could imagine was lying on a couch, talking to a wild-looking counselor with big hair and a yellow notepad, continuously writing frantic notes about me. If you're picturing Albert Einstein, that pretty much sums up the image in my head.

I also hesitated to see a counselor because, living in a small town, I didn't want to go to a counselor who might know the same people I did. I needed a safe place where I could share openly. I didn't want to feel like I was throwing anyone under the bus. Because of the relationship and ministry wounds I had experienced, I needed someone who could be completely objective, challenging, truthful, and empathetic.

It took some time, but after a while, I was able to find a professional Christian counselor about forty-five minutes away from our home. Initially, I thought to myself, *"Two or three visits should do it, and I'll be good."* Six months later, I finally wrapped up my last session with Lynn. Today, I look back and laugh at what I thought would be a short season of counseling, but, in the same breath, give thanks to God for those months that led to significant healing in my life. While it took longer than I anticipated, it was exactly what I needed to start moving past the painful things of the past and embrace the future—and my life—again.

If you find yourself continuing to struggle with depression, I encourage you to seek out a professional counselor. I'll be flat-out honest with you though: It's going to be hard work. And it often feels worse before it gets better. It may take longer than you think it should. Everyone's timeline of seeing a counselor is different and needs to fit with their personal experience and needs. However, no matter how long it takes, I encourage you to keep pushing through the pain and lean in to the discomfort. The peace that I found on the other side was so worth it.

Keep in mind that if you go to a counselor and it doesn't seem like a good fit, it's okay to continue looking until you find someone you're comfortable with. We all have different personalities, so finding a counselor who is compatible (much like a doctor) is important. However, make sure you're switching because you need a better fit, not because they are asking you to do the painful work of healing.

Self-care

Self-care is an area a lot of people struggle with. I know I did. As a wife and mom, I struggled with appropriate self-care for years. I spent so much time caring for others that I often put myself on the back burner. My eating, while not horrible, was not overly healthy. Exercise of any sort was almost non-existent, unless you count running after the kids.

Honestly, the thought of setting time aside for myself seemed selfish. As a wife and mom, I compared myself to images of other supermoms I saw on my social media feeds and chased that illusion like it was some award to be won. What I couldn't see was that their lives were often just as hurried and chaotic as mine, and many of the supermoms were as worn out and done as I was.

As a little girl, I still remember sitting in Sunday School and talking about having the J.O.Y. of the Lord in your heart. J.O.Y. stood for: *Jesus, Others, Yourself*. As a little girl, I understood that to mean that I needed to always put others before myself if I wanted to faithfully serve Jesus. And I wanted to faithfully serve Jesus, so I took it literally. Looking back, I realize that wasn't exactly the lesson my Sunday School teacher was trying to convey. However, it's the message I carried well into my adult years.

Today, I know that it should really read: J.Y.O. for *Jesus, Yourself, Others*. As selfish as that sounds, it's actually a more balanced and healthier way to approach life. As my mentor and friend Dan Miller says, "No one can pour from an empty cup." In order to serve and give to those around me, including my family, friends, employees, church, and beyond, I have to take time to fill up mentally, emotionally, physically, and spiritually.

It was during my pivotal moment of getting off the couch and taking that first walk around the field that I realized if I wanted to care for people well, I had to start taking care of myself. And when I care for myself, I actually give a gift to the people in my life because I can serve them from a full cup, not an empty one.

My Daily Self-care Today
Exercise

It all started with walking around the field but, eventually, as I felt better and had more energy, I started adding running to my days of walking. I was a high school track and cross-country athlete, so running was what I knew. In all honesty, I didn't have the energy or brainpower to figure out exercise that was any more complicated than that. In fact, I decided that I wasn't even going to join a gym until I could walk and run consistently for one year on my own. In previous years, I had joined a gym many times with the intention of going regularly; yet, somehow, I never found the time to actually step foot in the door. I knew walking and running were things I could do outdoors around my neighborhood, and that was free. It became a sort of challenge to see if I could meet that goal and each day I went out, it got a little bit easier.

At first, I just walked. Then I walked some more. Then, after a few months, walking turned into jogging, and eventually into running. I finally joined a gym two years later so I could take advantage of the weight training aspect, and I kept going with the running.

Three years after I started running again, I trained and completed my first half marathon. Six months later, I completed my second half marathon. I can tell you that I didn't run those races for the medal or recognition. I did it simply because I knew how vital exercise would be to help me stay healthy in body, mind, and spirit. Today that is the reason I run, hike, and mountain bike as much as I can. Exercise has been essential for keeping me from returning to the dark doors of depression.

Maybe running isn't your thing, and that's okay. What I encourage you to do is find some form of exercise that you can enjoy and stick with it. Find an accountability partner and start taking steps to a healthier you.

Here is what Dr. Michael Craig Miller, Assistant Professor of Psychiatry at Harvard Medical School, has to say about exercise and depression:

"Exercising starts a biological cascade of events that results in many health benefits, such as protecting against heart disease and diabetes, improving sleep, and lowering blood pressure. High-intensity exercise releases the body's feel-good chemicals called endorphins, resulting in the "runner's high" that joggers report. But for most of us, the real value is in low-intensity exercise sustained over time. That kind of activity spurs the release of proteins called neurotrophic or growth factors, which cause nerve cells to grow and make new connections. The improvement in brain function makes you feel better. In people who are depressed, neuroscientists have noticed that the hippocampus in the brain—the region that helps regulate mood—is smaller. Exercise supports nerve cell growth in the hippocampus, improving nerve cell connections, which helps relieve depression."[xi]

The Foods We Eat

The food we eat matters. If you have done any research about the power of food, you know that food can affect mood, determine energy (or lack thereof), and be a window into how we actually feel about ourselves. Before my depression, I didn't really think about my food choices. I made food, served it to my family, cleaned up the dishes, and called it a day. After my depression journey, I began to realize the power food had to heal our bodies. I realized that it had the power to not just fill me up, but to heal and to help me feel better about myself. Today, I have a certain regimen that I follow based on my own personal health goals and needs.

I am purposely not sharing the exact regimen that I use, only because I don't want you to get hung up on a particular program. What I encourage you to do is to start thinking about the food you're eating and how it might be affecting your current depression or anxiety. Take time to research nutrition and educate yourself about the food you are eating and the changes you need to make to be healthier in this area. If you're not sure where to start, seek out a qualified nutritionist or health coach and let them help you get started in the right direction. Besides helping you understand your food and map out a plan, they can also be a great source of accountability during this part of the process.

As an added benefit, when I started eating better, not only did it help my mental health, but it helped my emotional and physical health as well. It created a snowball effect because as I began to feel better from changing my eating habits, I began to have more and more motivation to work on other areas of my health, like exercise and sleep. Changes in those three areas alone became significant in how I was able to battle my depression, and they allowed me to make significant progress forward to where I am today.

Fun, Just Because

During one of my many sessions with my counselor, I remember Lynn asking me this simple question: *"Victoria, what do you do for fun? To relax? For the pure joy of it?"*

I began to rattle off my usual answers until she stopped me mid-sentence.

"No, Victoria. I mean, what do you love to do for fun? Not what your kids or husband want you to do for fun. What do you do for fun? To relax? To take care of you?"

And you know what? I could not answer her. I had no idea what I loved to do for myself. Nothing came to mind because it had been so long since I allowed myself to think about me. It had been years since I had been on a long hike, ridden my bike, or spent the day reading a book just because.

Her challenge to me that day was to think about the things that I loved to do. Then I was to do at least one thing for myself that week and report back to her at our next session. Those first weeks of figuring out what I loved to do were hard. Every time I came up with an idea, I shot it back down because it didn't seem practical or beneficial to anyone else. I was so used to helping everyone else that I couldn't imagine taking that time just for me. I knew guilt would eat me up, and I hated that uncomfortable feeling. You know the one I'm talking about? Like when you were a kid and snuck off with a book when you were supposed to be helping your mom with the dishes. Then your dad finds out you're not helping, and all of the sudden, you not only lose your book privileges but dessert before bed too.

That was me. But this time, I was an adult, just waiting for my dad to come around the corner and catch me reading when I should have been tending to all the adult things. That's why the first few weeks of Lynn's challenge were so hard. I had to relearn that it was okay to not only take time for myself, but to enjoy it as well. There's a novel thought! Enjoy what you do.

This is when I returned to hiking. And just like running, it was slow at first. Often Brian and I would go for a Sunday afternoon hike that took us two or three miles round trip. Today, it's not unusual for us to hike eight to ten miles at a time and absolutely love it. For me, there is something about the quiet of the woods that speaks to my heart and is deeply therapeutic. There, I feel like I hear from God best, and the rest of the world gets quiet for just a little while.

Changing the Conversation in our Heads

Self-care is not just about taking care of our bodies; it's also about taking care of our minds. That meant I needed to start taking the conversations I was having in my own head seriously. Often, we speak incredibly harsh words about ourselves and say things that we would never say to another person. Often I think to myself, *"If my husband or daughter were here right now, standing in front of me, would I say these things to them?"* The answer is always: *"Absolutely not!*" It would crush them; yet, the words I was choosing to speak to myself were no less impactful than if I were speaking them to my husband or one of my daughters.

That is why this verse in Philippians 4:6-7 (NLT) has become so important for me to remember so I can allow my heart and mind to stay Christ-focused instead of "me"-focused.

> "Don't worry about anything; instead, pray about everything. Tell God what you need, and thank him for all he has done. Then you will experience God's peace, which exceeds anything we can understand. His peace will guard your hearts and minds as you live in Christ Jesus."

This is what Paul was exhorting the believers in Philippi to do as well. He was challenging them to stay Christ-focused instead of others-focused and instructing them to turn their worries and concerns over to the only One who could give them true, lasting peace.

And while it may seem simplistic to say "just pray about it," that's exactly what I started doing. Whenever a negative thought came into my mind, I would make a conscious choice to stop the thought and pray, *"Jesus, help me know your truth. Help me understand and see the lie I am believing."*

Sometimes, though, the negative thoughts just kept coming. Just imagine you have spent years saying negative things continually. Those habit pathways for negative thinking are going to take time to replace. You literally have to give your thoughts a new track to run on. So when the negative thoughts just kept coming, I would take my next step. Change locations. If I was sitting in my house and struggling to think positive things about myself, I would grab my shoes, head for the park, and go for a run. Changing locations helped me move out of the negative place I was spiraling into and allowed a different perspective to take its place.

Often I would listen to worship music as I was walking or running. Remember, it matters what you choose to listen to in those critical moments. When we are feeling bad about ourselves, our first tendency is to put on music that matches our mood. However, just like everything else, this one is in your court. You are the driver of your thoughts. What you allow into your heart is what will manifest in your thoughts.

That's why another practical thing I did to help change the conversation in my head was writing out Scripture. I would take note cards and write down verses that encouraged me—ones that spoke about the way God saw me and reminded me of His love for me. I carried those cards around with me, putting them in my work bag, propped up in my car, taped to my computer screen and bathroom mirror. There is power in God's Word, but only if we are willing to read it, receive it, and apply it. Having a Bible sitting on your shelf does not mean that you know God's Word. You can't receive something you won't read and apply.

Intentional Rest

Intentional rest was not something I knew how to do prior to my depression. Of course, I went on vacation with my family and date nights with my husband. I occasionally went out with friends to the movies or attended a women's weekend retreat. Unfortunately, these occasions were few and far between, and they rarely felt restful. With trying to get a family ready for vacation—juggling all the things to take, packing the car, driving, arriving, unpacking, sand throwing, tantrum wielding, happyish family pictures, throwing it all back in the car—you arrive back home only to be exhausted from your vacation. In all seriousness, you now need a vacation from your vacation.

After the worst of my depression, when I began to really take charge of my health and practice better self-care, I realized that intentional rest was not just reserved for vacations and women's retreats but that it needed to be a part of my ongoing, daily practice.

Keep in mind that intentional rest is going to look a little different for everyone, but for me, that meant resting well at least once a week (usually on Sundays). On this one day, I purposely stay off my social media accounts, resist the urge to check my email, and rarely answer the phone, unless it's my kids or immediate family members. I attend church and then the rest of the day is spent hiking, reading a book, or taking a nap. The point is to do restful things that don't require me to rush or make me feel overwhelmed.

Sometimes intentional rest means sleep. In the early days, when my girls were tiny, I regret not taking time to nap when they did. Often I spent the time when they were napping rushing around, trying to get my long "to-do" list done before they woke up. That led to many years of being a tired and frazzled mom. I never gave myself permission to slow down and sleep when I needed to. If you're a young mom or dad reading this, and you feel you need permission to stop and sleep, I give you that permission. Take time to rest and get recharged. Your kids don't care if the dishes are done or if the house is perfect. What they care about is your ability to be present with them by taking care of yourself. Remember, we need to stop and refill so that we are pouring from a full cup, not an empty one.

Another way I intentionally rest is getting away once a quarter by myself. Up until a few years ago, I would have never imagined doing something like this. There would have been too much guilt involved and I would have worried about who was going to take care of everything. However, I have found that this getaway not only fills me back up, but it allows my kids and husband to practice their self-sufficiency skills (something for which they are more prepared than we give them credit for), as well as allowing them to be a blessing to their mom and wife. When was the last time you allowed someone to be a blessing to you? Let's not deny others the joy of giving because we are too afraid to receive.

During this two-to-three-day personal retreat, I spend time reading, journaling, writing, and planning for the next few months. I come back rejuvenated and ready to take on my responsibilities and be present for my family. I'm a better wife, mom, friend, and employer because of it.

Now, maybe a quarterly getaway is not something this is always possible for you in this season of your life. However, I would encourage you to take some time to brainstorm ways that you can incorporate intentional rest into your life and then add it to your self-care plan so that rest happens on a regular basis.

Daily Affirmations

Affirmation. According to Dictonary.com, affirmation means "the act or an instance of affirming; state of being affirmed." And, "the assertion that something exists or is true." [xii]

Did you know that affirmations are deeply powerful things? So powerful, in fact, that many successful business people point to them as a vital part of their success. They may quote positive affirmations first thing in the morning, speaking what they are choosing to see as true for their life. Affirmations such as: *"Today, I will bring the best version of myself to the day."* Or, *"Today, I am powerful, successful, and able to accomplish the things I set my mind to."*

To some, that might sound arrogant, or just a bit wonky. Crazy, you might think. But may I propose that every single person, you and me included, already speaks affirmations on a daily basis. The only difference is that ours may sound something like this: *"I'm so stupid. I can't ever get anything right. Nothing ever works out for me. Just wait until the other shoe drops. I'm not loved. I'm too broken. I will never beat this depression."* Every day, in our own minds, we review a script that we feel must be true of us and equally re-enforced by our life circumstances. And that kind of negative affirmation will continue unless we make a conscious choice to do something that helps counteract the negative affirmations we are saying to ourselves.

A healthy set of positive affirmations has become life-altering for me. As I started coming out of the worst of my depression and became conscious of my thought patterns, I realized that I had a poor habit of speaking negative affirmations to myself. When I realized what was happening, I made a choice to counteract those negative affirmations and practice speaking positive affirmations. I'll admit, it felt a little weird at first. I felt like a bit of an imposter because those things did not feel part of me yet.

Notice I said "feel." Remember that while our feelings are valid, they cannot always be trusted.

So, from the moment my feet hit the ground in the morning until I went to bed at night, I started using affirmations like this: *"I am fearfully and wonderfully made, I know that full well. I am a child of God, loved by my Creator and, as such, can utilize His strength to carry me through this day. For my fight is not against flesh and blood, but against the rulers and authorities of this dark world. I am more than a conqueror through Christ Jesus."* As you can see, mine were made of affirming Scripture that I was choosing to believe in advance of my feelings.

I challenge you to create a self-care habit of positive affirmations. Make a choice to replace the negative affirmations and then see what happens in your life over the next few weeks. Maybe you will choose to say them out loud while getting dressed in the morning, during your quiet time, sitting in the carpool line waiting for your kids or even write them out daily to help them stick in your mind better. No matter where it is, whether you choose to recite them to yourself or write them out, a daily habit of positive affirmation will go a long way in your battle against depression. You can find more daily affirmation examples at: www.victoriamininger.com/affirmations

Check-in Exercises

Has life ever been so full or overwhelming that you struggle to process what is really going on in your heart? Yes? Me too. In fact, I think we all have experienced those feelings at some point, whether you struggle with depression or not. Many times the busy nature of life can keep us hopping from place to place, leaving us very little space to process what is really happening in our hearts. Yet, if we want to make any forward progress on this road back to wholeness, I believe we need to take moments to at least pause and check in with ourselves.

A couple of practical ways I have learned to do that come from two different check-in exercises that were shared with me during a season of facilitating depression support groups at our church. Both of these allow you to check in and get a pulse on your current state of thinking and being.

The first one, the Heart Check-in Exercise, was shared with me when I spoke to a mom's playgroup one fall. As we all sat in a circle, the leader had each of us walk through the following heart exercise to focus on three specific things:

1. **Stillness:** Take a few minutes to quiet yourself, both physically and emotionally. This is best done by finding a quiet place, closing your eyes, and taking three deep, cleansing breaths.

2. **Vision:** With eyes still closed, fix your eyes on Jesus. Ask him to help you identify your feelings. Try to

only focus on one emotion that describes how you are feeling in that moment.

3. **Journal or Share:** If you are by yourself, simply take time to journal your thoughts. If you are in a group, share at any level of vulnerability you are comfortable with. Focus your journaling or sharing on the three questions below.

   a. Pick an emotion. How are you feeling based on what you identified during the vision part of this exercise? (happy, sad, overwhelmed, etc.)

   b. How are your relationships being affected?

   c. How is your relationship with God being affected?

This Heart Check-in Exercise is not meant to be a long, drawn-out process but rather an exercise that allows you to pause and check in with yourself before heading into further conversation with your group or any further reflection you might do personally. Keep in mind these ground rules if you are doing the exercise as a group: Listen to understand; Don't give advice unless requested by the person sharing; Let everyone have a time to share; Respect privacy, meaning everything shared in your group should stay in your group.

When we started using this exercise in our depression support group, I noticed a markedly positive shift in the group's engagement with one another and more participation in the overall discussion. Giving voice to each person and how they were feeling allowed others to see that they were truly not alone in their struggle.

Another great exercise that can be done individually is to keep a weekly mood chart. I first heard of this idea from one of our group participants, who mentioned that her counselor was having her keep a mood chart each week. Immediately, the group as a whole leaned in and wanted to know more. The participant went on to explain that her mood chart allowed her to track her daily moods. However, the power was not in filling out the mood chart but was in the ability it gave her to look back and evaluate her week. When she did, she often realized that her week wasn't as bad as she first thought. Instead, she was beginning to see pockets of good—pockets of hope and not despair. Tracking her mood began to give her the power to say, *"It's not as bad as I thought. I am making progress."* Seeing that kind of affirmation on paper is what can help propel us forward during a tough season, and I would challenge you to make your own mood chart and take a few weeks to track your progress. You might be surprised by the results.

You can download the Heart Check-in Exercise and a variation of the Mood Chart at: www.victoriamininger. com/selfcaretools

Accountability

When it comes to making a habit of self-care—visiting your counselor or doctor and implementing these healthy rhythms into your life—accountability to another person can go a long way in helping the habits take hold. I would encourage you to find a friend, or maybe your counselor, who you give permission to ask the hard questions and hold your feet to the fire.

Keep in mind though, if they do agree to hold you accountable, you must agree to respond kindly and not defensively. Our friends take a risk when we ask them to hold us accountable because implementing new habits and strategies can be uncomfortable and apt to make us grumpy. This is why my husband will never be my accountability partner. I love him enough to not put him through that. We've tried it before and have realized that it's not good for our marriage.

And remember, this journey doesn't have to look perfect. Let's stop romanticizing everything in our heads and simply get to the hard work of self-care. Let's do what it takes to fight forward every day. Healing is messy and hard. It's not Pinterest pretty. It takes grit and determination and a willingness to lean in to the reality of the work to see this battle through.

Daily Quiet Time/Prayer and Meditation

While a daily quiet time is the last self-care practice I am sharing with you, it is certainly not last on my list. In fact, a daily quiet time, where I spend time in worship, Bible reading, focused prayer, and journaling, is one of the very first things I do every morning, even on Sundays. If I want to be able to move through my day with strength, confidence, and a readiness to fight the lies that Satan wants to throw at me, then this is non-negotiable for me.

Of course, like all the other self-care practices I listed above, it takes willingness to make it a habit. It also takes willingness to get back up and start over when you fall off the wagon. It's going to happen. It happens to me. I'm extra tired and stay in bed longer than I planned. Or the kids remember, at the last minute, that they have to be at work in ten minutes and need a ride. (Cue bedhead and running out in my pajamas.) The phone rings early and work calls. Or, honestly, I just don't feel like it! Remember when we talked about not being able to trust our feelings? Yes, that would apply here too. The feeling is valid—but it's not trustworthy.

Making the daily choice to push through my feelings and take time for myself each morning is vital to the success of my day. It doesn't mean everything goes right, but I find that I am much better equipped to handle what the day holds when I take the time to be quiet and spend a few moments with God.

In Chapter 3, we talked about the importance of getting into God's Word on a regular basis. This quiet time is the exact place to start making that happen. Whether you take time in the morning, at your lunch break, or at the end of the day, I challenge you to make this self-care habit a vital part of your day as well.

If you're still not sure if you have what it takes to put some of these practical steps into place, allow me to share a pivotal point in my early depression journey that helped me take those first steps. Hopefully, it will help you too.

But I Just Can't

In the early months of my depression, as I lied on that old couch, I knew I needed to start doing something to get better. I knew I needed to see my doctor, possibly a counselor, and do something about my almost non-existent self-care habits.

But I was scared. Day after day I kept lying there, thinking to myself and arguing with God, *"But I just can't Lord. I just can't."*

Until, one day, I sensed this question from God: *"Victoria, you **can't** or you **won't**?"*

Talk about a slap upside the head. That was a hard one for me to hear because, honestly, I just wanted God to fix it. To unfurl a big banner in the sky mapping out exactly what to do and how long it would take.

However, His reply made me catch my breath. I believe that hearing that question was the beginning of realizing that no other human being was coming to my rescue. No one else could fix this for me. I needed to stand on my own two feet and fight for my healing and health. While I believe God is fully capable of reaching down and taking my depression away in an instant, that's not the path He allowed me to walk.

That's why, during key points in my journey, when I was struggling to take the next step, I would ask myself, *"Victoria, is it because you **can't** or you **won't**?"* It's hard to be brutally honest with yourself, isn't it? But sometimes that's what it takes for real change to take place. I knew that if I wanted to really heal, brutal honesty was what it was going to take. If I wanted to start walking out of this dark place, it meant sitting up and saying "I can!" and "I will!" to the steps I knew God was asking me to take—and then trusting Him for the results.

Setting Daily Habits

First of all, let me say that the only way I have successfully added good self-care habits to my life is by finding a daily rhythm for each of the habits I wanted to add. My daily rhythms and habits have become keys to helping me battle through and overcome the worst of my depression, and they are what allow me to continue operating in a healthy way even today.

I initially tried to incorporate these self-care habits without much of a plan. I knew they were good for me, but it was hard to stick to them when I wasn't sure what the end goal was. So, to start, I sat down with a blank journal and planned out my Ideal Day. I listed what time I would get up, when my quiet time would happen, where exercise fit in, how many hours would be focused on key work, when I would stop work and spend time with family and friends, and what my evening looked like so I could wind down and be ready for sleep.

I then, in the same journal, mapped out my Ideal Week in the same way. In my Ideal Week, I planned out the big pieces of my week and how I would want each day to play out. For instance, I know that for our family to run smoothly, I need time to take care of housework, bills, and grocery shopping. I also know that I need a certain amount of hours for connecting with team members at work and working with my coaching and mentoring clients. Just as important were times of rest and relaxation. All of that needed to fit into my weekly schedule. Therefore, one day a week I set aside as my family day, where I take care of certain family responsibilities and care for our home. The other days I have large blocks of work time that allow me to take care of my responsibilities in my businesses. The weekend is set aside for family time, Sabbath rest, and other miscellaneous things that need to be taken care of or events we want to enjoy. By mapping out my Ideal Day and

Week, I was able to see where the holes were in my plan and where I might be trying to do too much.

The key to planning Ideal Days and Weeks is to remember that they are ideal, not set in stone. Sometimes my days and weeks get close to my ideal, and other days those ideals get shot to pieces. It happens. You simply reset and start over the next day. I then review my Ideal Day and Week once a month to make sure nothing has shifted or needs to change based on what is on my plate that season.

When it came to specific rhythms, I also map those out just like I do my Ideal Day. While they are a part of my Ideal Day, I take time to plan them out a bit more in depth because of their importance to making the beginnings and ends of my days run smoother. For instance, I have a morning and evening rhythm that I stick to fairly closely. Each rhythm is about two hours in length. In the morning, I get up at the same time each day, shower and dress, come downstairs, and turn on the hot water for my tea. While the water is heating, I go out and feed the chickens and put the dogs out for the day. When I return, the water is usually ready for me to make tea. I then sit down and spend time in meditation and prayer.

The evening is similar. Two hours before I head to bed, I spend time relaxing with a book or watching TV or a movie with my husband. About an hour before bed, all electronics are turned off so that my body and brain start getting the message that it's almost time for bed. During that last hour, I read a book that is enjoyable but doesn't take a lot of thinking power. (I leave books that require thinking power for earlier in the day when my brain is less tired and better able to process.) Then the lights go out so I can get a full eight hours of sleep.

Just like Ideal Days and Weeks, my rhythms are not set in stone. Things happen. Kids come in late, a meeting runs over, a movie goes longer than expected, or I'm traveling and my normal schedule may be interrupted. However, the next day (or week, when I return home from traveling), I work at returning to my rhythms and practicing good self-care habits because doing so allows me to have a more focused and successful day instead of just randomly wandering through the week.

Keep in mind that your days and weeks will not look like mine. You have responsibilities that I might not in this season of life or your work schedule looks different than mine. I simply share what I have done to give you a practical example of what those Ideal Days and Weeks could look like as you work to map out your own rhythms and daily self-care habits.

One last encouragement to you, as you consider adding rhythms and habits to your day and week: Don't try to tackle them all at once. Rhythms and habits are best approached one at a time so that you don't get discouraged. All the self-care habits I listed above have taken me a few years to incorporate into my life on a regular basis. I would encourage and challenge you to simply pick one and get started. Once you have that habit down, then add another one. Stacking habits slowly will be key for your ability to implement them into your life.

For more inspiration, examples, and downloads on self-care, rhythms, Ideal Days, and Ideal Weeks visit: www.victoriamininger.com/selfcaretools

Your Turn

1. Is there any area in this chapter where you find yourself saying "I can't!" or "I won't!" How can you begin to take a step towards "I can!" and "I will!"?

2. What practical steps are you taking right now that have helped you in your depression journey?

3. What practical self-care step(s) do you need to start taking? What steps are the hardest for you to take?

4. What stood out to you about this week's reading? How might you apply it to your life this week?

This Week's Activity

Based on what you identified in question three, put at least one practical step into practice this week to help further your healing. Keep a journal of your progress. Remember, it doesn't have to be perfect. The point is to start. Record how it's going and how you are feeling while implementing this new practice.

CHAPTER 6

Help for the Hard Days

Have you heard that song by The Shirelles titled "Mama Said"? Yes, that song. Well, that is exactly what is running through my head right now as I sit and work on this chapter. Sometimes, I think it should be the theme song for the last few years of my life. While I have made incredible progress from the initial days of being diagnosed with clinical depression, anxiety, and mild PTSD, there are still days that are hard. Can I get an amen?

Over the years, I have read a lot of hope-filled books and articles on the subjects of anxiety and depression. And while many are encouraging and life-giving, they don't always talk about the hard days that can linger and raise their ugly heads again. And I don't want to be one of those people who makes you think that if you just do five steps, read your Bible, pray a lot, and have faith, you won't ever encounter a hard day, week, or month again.

The truth is, you will. Today, I still have to be incredibly vigilant to notice my own triggers. On occasion, I'll still have a panic attack. In those moments, I have to remember what my counselor taught me about breathing and verbally coaching myself back from a place where it feels like I'm dying. And those triggers and setbacks can be frustrating.

About six months after my depression diagnosis, I found myself in that place of frustration. I had hoped to be so much further in my journey than where I was. Sure, I could look back and see progress, but I was discouraged about not being further down the road. If you find yourself with the same frustration, don't get discouraged. It's completely normal to feel that way. We all do.

However, as time has marched on, I've realized this truth: Hard days do not invalidate all the work I've done up to this point or the work God has done in me. Remember that battling through depression is a process. It's a process that can still feel messy, jumbled, and exhausting, and just because you have hard days doesn't mean you won't have good days ahead.

On those hard days, I remind myself that I'm going to fall—and that's okay. The difference and indicator of progress will be in how I choose to rise from that fall. I didn't know it at the time, but even on that day when I was painting a house and the weight of depression brought me to my knees, I had to choose how I was going to rise. Granted, it took me a while to recover from that initial drop, but as I did, I knew the choice was mine to make. I had the power to say how this was going to end, how I was going to rise from this fall.

We all have a choice in how we rise. Yes, it might be shaky and incredibly hard at times, but it's always in our court. So, what do you do when it's hard? How do we find the strength to rise, move forward, and embrace the mess that is our stories?

First, we can take encouragement from the apostle Paul in the Bible. Paul knew a few things about struggling through hard things. In fact, the encouragement he shares comes after he experienced beatings, being shipwrecked, ridiculed, and imprisoned. He was a man who knew a thing or two about hardship and falling down. Yet, despite all he suffered, Paul knew the secret to finding contentment and trusting God in every circumstance. In Paul's day, Greek stoics saw contentment as an important virtue. However, Paul knew that true contentment, despite life's circumstances, comes from dependency on Christ—not one's self-sufficiency. In Philippians 4:11 (ESV), Paul says:

"For I have learned in whatever situation I am to be content. I know how to be brought low; and I know how to abound. In any and every circumstance, I have learned the secret of facing plenty, and hunger, abundance and need. I can do all things through him who strengthens me."

On the good days, I would embrace these verses wholeheartedly. Like that scene in *Rocky* where Rocky runs up the stairs in front of the Philadelphia Museum of Art, I would hold my arms aloft, pumping them in victory. I had overcome that day, and it felt good. A celebration seemed in order. Then, the bad days would hit again, and I couldn't hold my arms up, much less run up any stairs. My contentment with life was derived from how my day went rather than from the deep belief that God was for me, no matter the circumstances of my day.

The cycles of up and down, high and low, mountain and valley can wear a body out. Truly. So, how do we get off that roller coaster? How do we stretch out the good days and lessen the bad days? How do we find what Paul found—a contentment and trust in God—in all circumstances? I don't have an easy answer for you, but I do have some practical steps, things that I found helpful when I was battling hard days.

Shifting My Focus

Often, when we are in a negative place, we can find ourselves sitting and waiting for the other shoe to drop. Ever felt like that? As we sit there, if we are not mindful and we do not shift our focus to the positive, we run the risk of spiraling further and further down the dark rabbit hole of negativity, worry, and doubt.

How many days did I lie on that couch with my focus only on what I could not change instead of on what was in my power to do? It seemed the longer I lied there, the deeper my negative focus became ingrown and diluted of truth and reality. It wasn't until I made a conscious choice to get up and shift my physical and mental focus that I was able to slowly start taking steps out of that dark place. The truth is that what you focus on will grow. Our minds are incredibly powerful, and unless we willingly take control of our thoughts, we will continue to follow the same negative pathways over and over again.

Once again we return to Paul in chapter 4 of Philippians and his encouragement to the church at Philippi. At the beginning of the chapter, we read about two women in the church who were at odds with one another. Up until this point, both women had been "contenders of the faith." Their disagreement, which Scripture does not list, was causing division among the church at Philippi. That's why, in chapter 4, we see Paul exhorting the church in a number of ways surrounding this conflict, including Philippians 4:8 (ESV), which reads:

"Finally, brothers, whatever is true, whatever is honorable, whatever is just, whatever is pure, whatever is lovely, whatever is commendable, if there is any excellence, if there is anything worthy of praise, think about these things."

Instead of fighting with one another, Paul urges the church to think about things that would uplift and unify them. They had lost their focus, shifting away from Christ and not loving one another because of this disagreement in the church. That is why Christ urges us to renew our minds daily. He knows the secret to the peace and health of our minds and hearts is in direct correlation to what we think about and where we focus.

That is why, in Romans 12:2 (ESV), we find Paul writing to the church in Rome, urging the Christian community there to practical living with an inward focus. Some may even call it radical.

> "Do not be conformed to this world, but be transformed by the renewal of your mind, that by testing you may discern what is the will of God, what is good and acceptable and perfect."

How will we be transformed? By the renewal of our minds! That's powerful and amazing to me because that means that through Christ, I have the power to change my thoughts, which consequently control my ultimate outlook on life. However, it's not just about changing my thoughts for change's sake. If I want to be able to test and discern God's will for my life, renewing my mind daily is what it is going to take. Have you ever asked God: *What's your will for me God? What's my purpose?* A good way to find the answer to those questions is by renewing your mind daily so that you can hear from God; His will is truly the safest place we can ever be.

Replacing Lies with Truth

We talked about this just a few pages ago, but it bears repeating because it has become a powerful exercise in my own arsenal to fight depression. Whenever a negative thought begins to formulate in my brain, I have a choice. I can either entertain it—letting it stay through dinner and late-night tea—or I can check that negative thought at the door of my heart.

It can take a little practice, but the more you repeatedly hold up those negative thoughts to the lie detector of God's Word, the easier it gets to identify and dispatch them quickly. This can be tough at times because, remember, Satan masquerades as an angel of light, often telling us lies that have just a hint of truth in them. That's why having someone as a sounding board is so helpful. Sometimes being able to ask a trusted friend to keep you accountable can be a great way to gain another perspective.

I used to do this during many of my counseling sessions with Lynn. If I were really struggling in an area, I would ask, *"This is the negative thought I'm believing. Do you think it's true? If not, what am I missing? What is the truth I am struggling to hear instead?"* From her outside perspective, she could often see things that I couldn't, which allowed me the opportunity to shift my focus and replace the lie with truth. As you walk through your own season of counseling, I would encourage you to keep a journal in between sessions to write down the thoughts and questions that might come up as you're processing. Sometimes seeing your thoughts written out can also help you see the division between truth and the lies of the enemy. And as we bring those lies into the light of God's Word and truth, we have the opportunity to have our minds renewed so we can stop believing the lies and instead see the truth about what God says about us.

Letting Go of What I Can't Control

Written by the American theologian Reinhold Niebuhr, the Serenity Prayer often comes to mind when I'm struggling to let go of hard things.

> "God, grant me the serenity to accept the things I cannot change, courage to change the things I can, and the wisdom to know the difference."

For many years following the worst of my depression, I desperately wanted to go back and change a lot of things. I wanted to go back to people I had hurt, places where someone had walked away, and the moments I said "yes" when I should have said "no." To the days missed with my kids and husband and to the painful weight the depression placed on them. There was so much I felt responsible for—and so much that felt out of my control.

At some point though, I had to let go of the things and people I could not control. I had to trust that God was taking care of those situations and the people involved, that what He chose to redeem or not redeem was up to Him. I could not control people's willingness to forgive or what story they were choosing to believe about me. I could not control the gossip or others' rush to judgment about me or my family. I had to ask God daily to help me give up my expectations of what I hoped those relationships would be again and ask him to simply help me seek forgiveness where I needed to and allow him to restore relationship where he saw fit.

It can be hard to give up control, and it becomes a process just like many other things in this depression fight. Some days, it was about receiving forgiveness. Other days it was offering forgiveness. Some days, it was about making a conscious choice to halt the negative thinking and choose to see the positive, no matter how small that positive was.

Letting go of things I could not control has been a powerful piece of my depression fight and one of the most healing things for my mind and heart. It has become a daily exercise in trusting God, forgiving myself, forgiving others, and leaning into a life marked by depression.

Atmosphere is Everything

It's amazing to me how my surroundings can affect my mood. There are some days when sitting in my living room feels cozy, warm, and inviting, while other days it feels dark and smothering. Honestly, that atmosphere has more to do with what's happening in my head than the decor on the walls.

It's in those moments when the walls feel like they are closing in that I have a choice to make. Stay there to continue wallowing in negative thinking, or choose to create a change in my surroundings and perspective. Often, for me, that means grabbing my shoes and heading out for a walk down to the park or along our local greenway. Add in a bit of sunshine, fresh air, and people and the fog starts to clear away. Even when the weather is cold or cloudy, the fresh air somehow helps my thoughts get clearer, and I process my emotions and the hard day so much better than when I'm just sitting inside.

If I have the time, I might even head up to the mountain. We are blessed to live right at the foot of the Blue Ridge Mountains with the Appalachian Trail passing through the ridgeline above our town. Many times I have found my way to the long trail and hiked a few miles, eager to get to my favorite overlook or waterfall. The quiet and solitude soothes my heart, and I often feel closest to God in those places.

I challenge you to seek out those kinds of places for yourself—the places that make you feel like your heart and soul can breathe. That may not mean the mountains or the beach but a favorite corner of the local coffee shop or library. It's going to be different for everyone and each situation, but no matter the specific place, having that sacred spot is vital for helping us renew our hearts and minds.

Staying Consistent with Daily Habits

Whatever healthy daily habits you have been working on, don't let the hard days wipe them out. Stay consistent, because the good days are right around the corner. John Maxwell says, "You'll never change your life until you change something you do daily. The secret of your success is found in your daily routines." All the things I listed under self-care in Chapter 5 are part of my daily rhythm and habit routines today.

Consistent daily routines were something I never put in place until after my depression. Before, I just ran through my day like my hair was on fire and barely got through by the skin of my teeth. No wonder I crashed so hard. It wasn't until after the worst of my depression that I knew I not only had to slow down, but I had to become intentional about my days. Without intentionality, we are like a wave in the ocean, tossed here and there by whatever wind or current comes along.

By bringing rhythm and order to my days, I was able to find calm and peace in some of those daily routines during the hard days. As I shared before, I have a set time I get up every morning. Once I get up, I go to the kitchen, turn on the kettle for my morning tea, grab my vitamins, and then slip out to feed the chickens and put the dogs out while the water heats up. Then, I settle in with my tea and spend time in worship, prayer, and Bible study. Once those routines are complete, I jump into my workday, whatever it holds.

If I miss my morning routine because I overslept or gave in to the mindset that skipping my routine wouldn't matter, I feel it later in the day. Sometimes physically, but often mentally and spiritually even more. How my morning goes, so goes my afternoon.

It's important that I stay consistent. Consistency with my daily habits is one of the key things that made it possible for me to launch my own company in 2016 and to write this book. The reality is that we get more done with intentionality than when we choose to just wing it. Daily habits matter, especially on the bad days. And once you get consistent and those daily rhythms become deeply ingrained habits, it becomes less of a hard choice to stick to the rhythms and more automatic, even on the hardest days. The benefits and long-lasting effects on your life from the right daily habits make the effort to create them worth it.

Keep Leaning into the Discomfort of Healing

Healing from anything is rarely comfortable. The reality is that we did not get to this place of depression overnight, and we will not heal overnight. There are going to be hard conversations, painful discoveries, tears, laughter, and pain. It will be uncomfortable. Often we find ourselves running from the discomfort, but until we are willing to face it, we will keep spinning our wheels in the same place. There has to be a point when you are willing to get up and fight for your life.

I remember when I was meeting with my counselor she would ask me if I wanted to keep pushing through the hard stuff. There were some sessions I left exhausted and drained from processing some really hard things. So much of me wanted to give up. To just say, *"Forget it!"*

But I knew deep down that if I wanted to keep moving forward, and if I wanted to really heal, I had to face the hard things. Each time she asked me if I wanted to keep going, I responded, *"Yes, I've got to keep going. I don't want to stop short of the finish line."*

Years ago, when I was a sophomore in high school, I took first place in the local cross-country meet. Up until that point, I was an unknown runner who had never won a race in her life. I had placed before but never captured that elusive first place medal.

When I toed the starting line of that race, I had no idea what the race would hold that day. When the gun went off and the swarm of girls took off down the road, I fell comfortably back into the middle of the pack. I knew there were much faster runners that day, and I had no expectations that I would place, much less win. However, for some reason, that day I decided that I would push myself as fast as I could. In previous races, I often slowed my pace when my legs started hurting because hurting legs are not comfortable. I wasn't ready to push through that kind of pain. But, that day, I decided ahead of time that I was going to push through the pain no matter what. I wanted to be a better runner, and I knew pushing forward was the only way to get there.

And the pain came about two miles in. However, since I had already decided to push through, I kept going. I can be bullheaded like that.

Soon, I found myself all alone somewhere behind the pack of the four lead girls with the other half of the pack somewhere behind me. The woods I was running through were strangely quiet, and I had to keep coaching myself mentally not to slow down.

As the last quarter mile approached, I topped a small hill and caught sight of the front pack. I was surprised to find myself so close to them. That had never happened. It was at that moment I decided I would try to run just a bit harder and see how close I could get to them—just for fun. I picked up the pace, and the distance began to close.

About 100 meters from the finish line, my coach appeared beside the course. *"You've got 'em! You've got 'em! Kick it in now! Kick it in now!"* I had learned to listen to my coach despite my aching legs. If coach told you to run, you ran.

In the last fifty yards, I hit an all-out sprint with the distance closing even faster. Along the course, the crowd was cheering and yelling at the other runners, *"She's coming, she's coming, you better move!"* However, they must have thought the crowd was joking because they never picked up their pace. The last time they had glanced back there were no other runners in sight.

By the time I caught them at twenty yards, I was moving so fast that I startled them as I passed. Two of them tried to surge, but it was already too late. I had passed them and crossed the finish line, taking first place. I don't know who was more shocked: them or me. From that day forward I was known as "Victoria, where did she come from, Gomez." (My maiden name.)

In that race, I had a choice to make. Stay where I was comfortable or push through the pain and reach for the finish line. I have to admit that, until the last twenty yards, I had no idea how that race might end. There was no promise that even if I pushed that hard that the race would end in my favor. But I had to try. I had to trust that my training and all my coach had taught me would come together in that critical moment.

Obviously, you can only take the analogy of that story but so far. The point I'm trying to make is this: Growth and change only happen when we are willing to lean into the discomfort that it brings. If I had slowed down at all because of the dreaded pain in my legs, I would have never won that race. To this day, I am so glad that I pushed through the pain that day. Because of that race, because I dared to challenge myself, I would go on to become a much stronger runner throughout the rest of my high school career, not to mention the lesson I carried with me for my battle with depression.

The Value of Pain

Just like leaning into discomfort of growth has value, pain itself has value if we are willing to let it be our teacher, especially on the hard days. Pain has the ability to develop us, to produce maturity and refine our hearts and minds, if we allow it to. More importantly, it has the ability to refine our faith and strengthen our direct relationship with God.

Today, my faith and relationship with God are at an entirely different level than they were before my depression. For that, I am grateful. In what has become my life verse, we read this in James 1:2-4 (NIV):

"Consider it pure joy, my brothers and sisters, whenever you face trials of many kinds, because you know that the testing of your faith produces perseverance. Let perseverance finish its work so that you may be mature and complete, not lacking anything."

This might be another verse that you wrestle with like I did—in particular, the first part, where it talks about joy in trial. Seriously? Joy? Yet, I believe that what James is talking about is our response and approach to trial and pain. If we go into it with disbelief while grumbling, all we get back is bitterness and resentment. But if we approach it with grit, grace, and faith, the results will be vastly different. Keep in mind that the *testing* of our faith does not *produce* faith. If we have no faith going into our trials, we will not magically produce it. However, if we have a faith in Christ prior to the trial, that trial refines what is already there and produces a deeper, stronger, more resilient faith.

So what does produce faith? Romans 10:17 (ESV) tells us:

"So faith comes from hearing, and hearing through the word of Christ."

In other words, faith is built in us as we hear, receive, and understand the Word of God in our lives. Remember when we talked about the power and purpose of God's Word in our lives back in Chapter 3? It is through the power of God's Word that we find strength to walk through trials and find healing.

God's Word is the foundation we build on so that everything we do—exercise, eating well, seeing our doctor, talking to a counselor, and good self-care—works together to form a holistic response to the fight against depression. The reality of depression is that hard days are still going to come. It's not a matter of if but when. Being prepared for the hard days is what helps us make forward progress in our daily fight. Building a strong foundation in God's Word is what keeps the rest of the house from cracking and shifting over time. This foundation holds everything together—even when the world feels like it is falling apart again.

Your Turn

1. What is your current response to hard days? Is it a positive or negative response?

2. If it's negative, what is one thing you can do to help change that response to a positive one? If it's positive, what is one thing you can add that might help you grow more in that response?

3. What is one thing that can trip up your positive response to a bad day?

4. What is one practical step you can add to your tool belt that would help you move forward on bad days?

5. What stood out to you about this week's reading? How might you apply it to your life this week?

This Week's Activity

Take time this week to map out a "It's a Hard Day" plan. Write out ways you will choose to be kind to yourself, the self-care that needs to happen, and how you will communicate with those around you. With a plan in place, facing hard days can lose some of its sting. Share your plan with a loved one or with a close friend so you have an ally as you fight to rise well.

Friends are angels that lift us to our feet
When our wings have
Trouble remembering how to fly
–AUTHOR UNKNOWN

CHAPTER 7

Re-engaging in Life

I remember the first time I tried to go back to church. It was terrifying. Not because of the people but because of the memories it evoked. Painful memories have a way of haunting our minds and hearts beyond even what I can understand sometimes. They keep us grounded in the past, refusing to let us move forward to a hopeful and vibrant future. Our family had gone to church sporadically the summer following my husband's resignation from being a pastor. I remember feeling relief every time we had Sunday plans that kept us from stepping foot in the sanctuary. The Sundays we did make it to church left me exhausted, mentally and physically. It was an experience unlike any I had faced before.

Even though our church had given us a three-month sabbatical at the onset of my depression and sent us for restorative counseling with a wonderful couple in Georgia, my husband and I both knew that it wasn't going to be enough. What we had both hoped would be a short-lived season was turning into a much longer battle.

Knowing that I was going to need a lot more time, my husband made the choice to resign from his role as a pastor so that we could focus on getting better as a family and a couple. However, when he stepped down from leading, it naturally changed our relationships and the community we gathered with. Add to that a depression that drove me to isolation with no desire to be with people at all and we had a recipe for ongoing disconnection.

In the initial season of my depression, large crowds were difficult for me and often caused me to panic and run for cover. Getting to know new people was simply out of the question. I spent many days worried that I would never get over the panic so easily triggered by things that used to feel safe and normal. It also made me deeply sad about the profound loss I felt of a community I had been a part of for over twenty-five years. Isolation is what I craved, but isolation was also slowly killing me.

As I shared earlier in this book, while our depression can drive us to seek isolation, the thing that we need most (the thing that will speed our healing) is the presence of healthy and trustworthy people. If you're in that place right now, of needing healthy and trustworthy people, know that it's okay if it takes time to search them out and build relationship. It's important to remember that not all people are safe or healthy for you in the season you are in. It's appropriate and okay that you take time to know someone before confiding in them deeply.

I am thankful that after some intentional work with my counselor and time to process and heal some of my wounds, I reached a place when I was ready to re-engage with people in communities that I used to enjoy.

But I was worried about the panic attacks that were still present and that flight response that overtook my mind whenever I felt unsafe. I took those worries back to my counselor because I knew I needed to get over this hurdle if I was ever going to move forward, re-engage in life, and start leading again. During our sessions, Lynn began to coach me on how to re-engage with others in a way that would help me make progress, but would also help address the panic attacks and feelings of social overwhelm and anxiety.

She explained it to me like this: *"Because of some of your past traumas, any time you get near a crowd of people, your body goes into a fight or flight mode. This is a normal response that happens when you are actually in danger. However, in someone with PTSD or those who suffer anxiety or panic attacks, this response can trigger any time we hear, see, or smell something that reminds us of the past trauma, triggering your body to run away even though you're actually safe. The only way to start overcoming and short-circuiting this response is to continue approaching the things that trigger an attack in order to reset your brain and its response."*

And that made sense to me. I most certainly wanted to re-engage in community, but at the rate I was going, I might as well have gone to live on an island. So, I started approaching the things I was afraid of. Like going places that made me nervous or had triggered panic attacks in the past. And that was hard beyond belief. Every fiber in my being screamed to run away, but my desire to start living again screamed louder. Some might call that brave; I call it daring to fight.

And the triggers came in places like churches, large and small gatherings of women, conferences, and even business meetings. Initially, no one felt safe, and I would feel the panic rising along with my heart rate. Outwardly you couldn't tell anything was wrong. Internally the battle raged forward, the enemy daring me to cross the front line. I like to think I took him by surprise each time I dared to step forward. Dared to approach that which frightened me. And each time I dared, I took a little more ground.

Initially I would only go somewhere if my husband or children were with me. They were safe, and I knew that I could hold my husband's hand the entire time if I needed to. Sometimes we would make it to the parking lot of the church, and I could feel my heart racing, chest tightening, hands shaking, and my head would swim with stars and lights. Brian got really good at noticing when I was struggling, so he would send the girls ahead of us and sit with me in the car as I worked through my breathing.

Once I had a handle on the panic, we would step away from the car and face the crowd together.

At first I could only sit in the back of the church or a meeting, checking to see where the exits were just in case I needed to slip out. During those days, weeks, and months of facing my panic, I didn't hear a word of the sermon or lesson. I can't remember singing or the people I met. Over time though, as I faced those places and people, working through the panic and anxiety, I was able to sit in the middle of the church. Eventually, I even made it to the first few rows. At times, I would have setbacks and find myself only comfortable with the back row again. But slowly, the panic began to subside and my ability to work through each episode gradually became stronger. Five years later, I rarely have a panic attack and enjoy being with people and engaging in new communities. I travel regularly by myself, attend conferences, and lead team and company meetings. I can sit in large crowds and am part of several smaller communities that I enjoy and continue to build strong relationships in. Honestly, it feels nothing short of amazing. Even my husband comments about how awesome it is to see me lead so strongly with a greater sense of confidence than I ever have before.

And I think that is the true power of our trials. Refining fires strip away the unnecessary and reveal what has always been below the surface. Seeing my struggle and pain through that lens helps me start making sense of the road

I have travelled. It doesn't mean I understand it all, but my heart is at peace knowing it was not all wasted. As it says in Isaiah 48:10 (ESV):

"Behold, I have refined you, but not as silver; I have tried you in the furnace of affliction."

And through Christ's mercy and grace, he met me in that furnace. He did not abandon me to the flames but instead stood with me in the fire and smoke. And just when I thought I might be consumed, he carried me out. Changed? Yes. Scarred? Beyond belief. Hopeless? Never. Restored? Absolutely!

The Power of Community

Re-engaging in community can be hard. I get that, because I lived it. However, I know that if I really want to be able to heal and fight forward each day, I need a healthy and trustworthy community. If you find yourself continually isolated from people, your battle will be that much harder. God created us to be in relationship with others. He created us to thrive and find help, love, and belonging in community. Yet, because so many of us have been hurt by people and communities, our level of trust is low or non-existent.

So how do we re-engage in community and with individual people in a healthy way? Here are three practical ways I began to re-engage in community:

1. I identified which communities I desired to be a part of and then looked for healthy versions of those communities. For our family, that meant re-engaging in church and finding a faith family that would love and challenge us to grow, offer a safe place for continued healing, and ultimately be a place we could serve again.

2. Identifying one or two ladies I wanted to get to know and felt I could be comfortable with. I would invite them to coffee and spend time getting to know them and their stories. Sometimes these relationships flourished and other times they were for a season. But each one helped draw me back into community at a rate my heart could handle.

3. I sought out an intentional mastermind group. A mastermind is simply a peer-to-peer group comprised of individuals with similar interest that gathers in support, to give input, challenge one another, and share life together. Sometimes, these groups meet locally or gather online, with in-person events or retreats a few times a year. I have been part of three different masterminds over the last few years, and each one has been just what I needed in that season and has added significant community to my life.

So, how do you know if a community or person is healthy and safe? Honestly, the best way I know how to tell if someone is healthy is to look at the fruit of their lives. If they profess to be a Christian believer, what is the fruit of their walk with Christ? I'm not talking about perfection, but how do they carry themselves? How do they treat other people? How do they talk about other people (or not talk about other people)? How do they care for other people? Every person's life speaks for itself, good and bad.

Brené Brown, a shame researcher and one of my favorite authors, says this about sharing your story with others:

> "When we're looking for compassion, we need someone who is deeply rooted, is able to bend and, most of all, embraces us for our strengths and struggles. We need to honor our struggle by sharing it with someone who has earned the right to hear it. When we're looking for compassion, it's about connecting with the right person at the right time about the right issue."

You will know you're in a healthy community of people when there are those you can tell your story to who can hold space for you in that place as you heal and grow. They won't share it with everyone around them or offer it as "prayer request gossip" but will wait until you're ready to share your own story. They can be trusted to be a true confidant in your life.

As I mentioned before, searching out these kinds of people and communities takes time, as well it should. Be bold enough to ask God to show you who to approach and which communities to participate in and then give it time.

Sharing Your Story

Sharing your story can be its own kind of therapy and another way to engage in community. However, done the wrong way, at the wrong time, it can cause more harm than good, both to others and yourself. So how do you know when you're ready to really share your story beyond just a select few? Maybe you hope to use the pain you experienced to help someone else in a similar place. Just recently I saw this quote from author and speaker Jon Acuff that summed it up for me beautifully:

> "The scars you share become lighthouses for people who are headed for the same rocks you hit."

And he's right. If my story can be a lighthouse to another, I've asked God to use it. Truthfully, I wasn't sure I would ever want to share it. And if I did, how was I going to know I was ready? I remember asking God that exact question about a year before I started working on this book because I was honestly scared about not getting it right. It's funny when you ask God for something and he answers in a way you weren't exactly expecting. I prefer banners in the sky and a direct phone call wouldn't hurt. Instead, he sent me a podcast.

Often when I'm walking, on one of my longer runs, or traveling in my truck, I spend time listening to podcasts on a variety of subjects. That day, as I jogged our local greenway, I was listening to Michele Cushatt and Kathi Lipp on their Communicator Academy podcast. I love their podcast because they talk about speaking, writing, and the overall art of communication. That episode, the ladies were answering listener questions about stories and communication. Guess what the question was that day? *"How do you know you're ready to share your hard story?"*

Coincidence? I think not.

Having listened to Kathi and Michele for some time, and having read Michele's book, *Undone: A Story of Making Peace With An Unexpected Life*, I knew these ladies were intimately acquainted with hard things and difficult battles. Both bore the scars of their journey, and I leaned in for Michele's reply:

"You will know you're ready to share your story when you are able to touch the scars of your story and they no longer bleed or ooze. There will be a day where you can touch that scar and remember but not wince in pain. That is when you know you are ready."

And in that moment, God answered the exact question I had been seeking an answer to. That's when I knew I was ready. After traveling the hard years of depression, battling hard to find healing, I finally felt ready to share my story. The wounds had been treated and allowed to heal. No longer were they just scabbed over; I bore a permanent scar that told of the road I had traveled—and survived.

And just like me, you too have a story to share. Every single one of us does, in fact, and each is equally important. Yet, so often we discredit our stories because they don't sound like someone else's story. We make excuses because maybe our story doesn't feel as dramatic as their trial, heartache, or experience.

The truth is, telling our stories was never meant to be a competition. It's in sharing and hearing each other's stories that we find commonality, compassion, and life once again. Telling your story may just be the beacon of hope someone else needs during their most painful moments. It's okay that it doesn't look perfect, that it feels messy sometimes, and that not everyone will understand or receive you. Remember that they are in the middle of their own stories, and not everyone is meant to travel with you.

Daring to fight for your life…it's hard. I wish there was a different truth I could speak, but that would serve no one. Instead, learn to lean in to community and the discomfort of engaging with people again. Learn to lean into the sometimes uncomfortable work of hearing another's story. It may be the very beacon of hope you need for your own journey.

Re-engaging as a Leader

Today my life seems to be defined as "before" my depression and "after" my depression. It was such a significant season in my life that it couldn't help but change me. The person I was before is not necessarily the person I am after. Before my depression, I was known as being a really outgoing person, always being available, and being a master of multitasking. Today, that is not necessarily true. I'm still outgoing and I love being with people, but I know I'm a bit more reserved and tend to be a bit more contemplative these days. Often, when I spend a lot of time with people, there is a point when I have to pull back and take some time to recharge alone. I can spend hours by myself, not because I'm avoiding people, but because that's how I recharge and take care of myself now. I no longer say "yes" to every request. It's not because those requests are bad. In fact, many of them are worthy causes. However, I have learned that when I say "yes" to something, I'm saying "no" to something else. I don't want a "yes" to be at the expense of the things that matter most to me, like my husband and daughters, my faith, and my overall health.

Does saying "no" put you at risk of others being upset or mad at you? Absolutely! Many folks, not knowing my story, don't always understand why I say "no" and keep so much margin in my life. But that's okay. I don't need them to understand. I know what it's like to say "yes" too much, and I've suffered the consequences for it. And, honestly, I'm not willing to make that mistake again for anyone and risk my mental, emotional, physical, and spiritual health like I did before. The price is way too high for being able to say I am socially accepted by those around me. For a recovering people pleaser like myself, my depression was a huge wake-up call, and I choose every day to heed its warning and the painful lesson it taught me.

And trials, like depression, can do that. They can teach us and change us, if we allow them to. When we go through a refining fire, it begins to reveal what is truly underneath. I can't say I liked everything this trial revealed in me, and I have had to work on my own heart issues along the way. It not only revealed things in me but also significantly changed the way I lead today.

When the worst of my depression was over, and I was ready to re-engage in life and leading, I had no idea where to start. The leader I was before was not the leader I wanted to be going forward. I was going to need to set healthy boundaries. I would need to learn how to respond to people differently and lead them forward without taking on all their problems. The old way, of flying by the seat of my pants and saying "yes" to everything, was not going to work. I felt stuck.

My depression battle had stripped me of so much strength and energy that I felt weak and vulnerable. Yet, my heart desired to lead again, to step into the arena of life and engage with the people around me. I admit I spent a lot of time searching Google for "getting started after a difficult season." I think many of us wish all answers could be found on Google. However, the answer to my questions was deeper than Google could answer.

Maybe you're a recovering leader like I was. Maybe you've wondered how to start stepping back into the arena of leading. That's why I decided to include this piece, because I know I am not the only one. And while I don't have it all figured out yet, I thought it might be helpful to share some of the steps that I took to re-engage in leading others again.

The first place I started on my journey back to leading was asking myself some key questions and taking definitive steps.

1. **Asking: Where and who do I want to lead?** It took a while for me to answer that question. I wasn't necessarily interested in leading where I did before. However, I was giving a lot of thought to stepping into an area I had never considered before: building and running my own company with the hopes of growing it to be a place of meaningful work in a life-changing environment for others. I knew I didn't want to just be a solopreneur but that I wanted to be an employer who could provide work to those needing a place to grow, maybe even start over in life, and help them achieve their own personal goals and dreams. I didn't just want to build stuff, but to truly build people.

2. **Meeting with a leadership coach:** Once I identified where and how I wanted to lead, I took time to meet with a leadership coach. Yes, it meant investing time and money into that resource, but, for me, it was worth it to gain clarity and have them help me map out a direction so that I could gain ground in this area. And while I couldn't see how the whole thing would play out, I knew getting started was one of the biggest hurdles.

3. **Investing in my own personal and professional growth:** The third thing I did was start investing in my own personal and professional growth again. I started reading a ton of books on every subject. I listened to podcasts and leaned in to what others were teaching. That didn't mean I implemented everything I heard. You still have to use discernment in that process and figure out what works for and fits your current journey. But those days, weeks, and now years of intentional growth have been key in helping me run my own business and helps me to lead and grow others that come through our company.

4. **Investing in a Mastermind:** I knew a mastermind was where I could and would be challenged and supported as I built my company and moved back into a place of leadership. As I shared earlier, a mastermind is simply a group of like-minded individuals that come

together to help and challenge one another to grow in a specific area such as in business or simply to share life together. Some Masterminds meet locally, while others are spread out nationally and come together a few times a year to meet in person during a weekend retreat. Today I can honestly say that being a part of a mastermind has been key to my growth both personally and professionally.

And while the road has not been smooth, or even predictable, leadership is a place that I have grown back into overtime. Today, what started out as a small construction cleaning business in 2016 has morphed into a full-fledged construction firm serving the residential market in building amazing backyard structures and spaces. But beyond building stuff, what I am most excited about is our ability to build people. As of the writing of this book we have a staff of twenty-nine and anticipate more growth in the years to come. Honestly, nothing brings me greater joy than seeing our men and women growing personally and professionally, affecting change in their lives and the lives of their families for generations to come. It's amazing to me how God has taken the initial desire I had and done more with it then I could have ever dreamed possible.

I don't know that I ever imagined being the founder and CEO of a construction company. It's a bit of a rare thing for a woman to fill that spot, but it's the path and door God has opened for me. Often I have thought that my husband should be the one to fill the CEO role, and, most certainly, he is an integral and driving force of the business. In fact, I don't like referring to it as "my business," even though legally that is what the paperwork says. The reality is that we both run this ship and he is a vital part of this team God has put into place today. He fills the role of dreamer and visionary and leads our marketing and sales force, while I operate as the integrator of our company, making sure the day to day operations of our company run smoothly across all our teams and divisions. Honestly, it's been a bit of a wild ride back to leading, but because of the lessons I learned through my depression battle, I am able to implement holistic practices that keep me balanced as I lead. That, I believe, is a testament to the healing power of a mighty God.

Maybe as you're reading this book, you are not quite ready to re-engage with others. Or maybe you've tried and it hasn't gone well. Don't get discouraged. I believe as you continue to fight forward in this journey of depression, you will reach a place where you want to re-engage. It won't be easy, but I believe re-engaging with community is a vital piece of returning to a fulfilling and vibrant life. Remember, you don't travel the road alone. As Jon Acuff says, "Never compare your beginning to someone else's middle." In other words, don't judge the progress of your journey by someone else's. Just keep your eyes focused on the best next step and, in time, you will be able to re-engage and find life again.

Your Turn

1. Where do you need to re-engage in community?
    Or, if you have re-engaged in community, what
    need is that community meeting for you?

2. If you haven't re-engaged in community, what might be
    holding you back? Can you identify the feeling or maybe
    something that happened to cause fear of re-engaging?

3. Can you identify a community or one or two people
    you know who could be helpful to reconnect with in
    your ongoing journey?

4. Is it time to share your story? If not, what places are still bleeding that might need additional healing? If you're ready, who has earned the right to hear your story as it is right now?

5. What stood out to you about this week's reading? How might you apply it to your life this week?

This Week's Activity

What is one thing you can do this week to re-engage in healthy community? Maybe it's a small group at church or having coffee with a friend. Once you have identified how to re-engage, take the step to make it happen this week.

See, I am doing a new thing!
Now it springs up; do you not perceive it?
I am making a way in the wilderness
And streams in the wasteland.

–ISAIAH 43:19 (NIV)

CHAPTER 8

Today and Beyond

One of the most frequent—and whispered—questions I receive from those who are battling their way through depression is this: *"Does it ever get better? Do you think you will ever not battle depression?"*

And really, they are not asking the question so much for me as they are for themselves. There is this worry that sits in the back of our minds when it comes to depression, a worry about whether it will ever really get better. Will there ever be a day that we wake up and don't feel like the weight of the world is sitting squarely on our shoulders, taunting us to just stay in bed? Will there ever be a day when life feels normal and doesn't take so much effort to get through?

That's the real question. Will I ever feel better? Will I ever conquer this depression? Will the days get any easier?

These are real, honest, and valid questions. Questions that deserve an honest and straightforward answer. As I have endeavored to do throughout the pages of this book, I will shoot straight with you. My answer to that question is this: I honestly don't know.

While that is probably not the answer you were hoping for, I feel that it is the most honest one I can give. The reality is that every single person is different and uniquely made. As such, every person will respond differently to medications, counseling, dietary changes, an exercise regimen, or other ways of battling depression.

In the same breath, I can also truthfully say with full conviction that I believe God can reach down and choose to heal us completely. So completely that we never, ever struggle with depression or anxiety again. While that has not been my story up until now, I still pray for that and believe it can happen.

However, I personally do still battle depression and anxiety at times. I still have to watch how much I carry on my plate. Large crowds can still be tough for me, as well as intimate groups of people. When I feel my stress levels rising, I know it's a signal that I'm reaching my limit, and I have to adjust accordingly. However, just because I still battle depression and anxiety does not mean life has stopped for me.

Implementing the daily practices and strategies that I shared in this book has helped me live a very full life. I dared to fight and take my life back. I am no longer paralyzed by my depression, anxiety, or panic attacks. Today I spend time overseeing the day to day operations of my company and heading up team development and training for our teams. I speak to large and small groups a few times a year. I've finally returned to writing on a regular basis, and, most importantly, I am able to spend quality time with my husband and daughters.

I don't share all that to say, "look at me." I share that to say that even if your depression never fully goes away, there is still an amazing and full life to be lived. There is hope for the future! My prayer is that you will experience a complete and full healing from depression and anxiety. That will always be my prayer for you.

So what now? Where do you go from here? Great question! While there can be a lot of different answers to those questions, I am going to close with three key areas that have helped me as I go through each day of my own journey.

Serving Outside Ourselves

"You have not lived today until you have done something for someone who can never repay you."
– JOHN BUNYAN

These words from John Bunyan are so true for me. There is something about helping someone else that changes how I view life. All of the sudden, the worries I carry with me diminish when I'm focused on the needs of another. In particular, helping those who have no way to repay me, even if they wanted too.

About three years ago, my daughter, Rachel, and I joined a small team of volunteers and headed to the beautiful state of West Virginia. Just the year before, several small communities had experienced devastating floods that wiped out homes and took the lives of a number of people in the community. Mennonite Disaster Service had been on-site for the last year bringing relief and were helping to rebuild homes that had been swept downriver.

Throughout that week, we rose early to eat and receive our work assignments before heading out for a day of swinging hammers, putting up drywall, and framing rooms. The work was hard and tiring. At the end of each day, we arrived back at the makeshift headquarters to shower, eat dinner, and collapse into our beds, grateful for a few hours of sleep before starting again. Yet, no matter how tired we were, the group worked with joy and comradery, which kept our tired and aching muscles moving.

As we neared the end of the week, I was helping hang the last of the drywall in a tiny, but cozy, house. The previous structure had been washed completely off its footings and sent crashing down a usually peaceful stream turned raging river. It now flowed lazily a mere 100 yards away, looking almost picturesque in the late afternoon light.

A gentle knock sounded on the newly hung front door. With barely any hesitation, the door swung open, and a young lady followed by an elderly gentleman stepped across the threshold. They glanced around, smiles lighting their faces, and, with a nod of their heads, said, *"Looking good, looking good."*

Calling everyone to the living room, our foreman introduced us to Joe. This was to be Joe's new home. For the last year, he had been living with family, squeezing into an already crowded house. In a few short weeks, he would be back in his own place, with a new space to call home and settle once again. You could see the joy on his face mixed with the sadness over what had been lost.

His life had been spared, but the old life he had known was gone. Swept away with the rain and a raging river. For a few moments, I connected with that pain. Connected with the joy of new life and the sorrow over what had been before. With that connection, my heart healed a bit more that day. Here was another who had suffered loss, grief, and death. Here was another who was bravely rebuilding. Here was another who was forging ahead into a new life with grit, grace, and faith.

He couldn't repay any of us, at least not monetarily. Instead, payment came in the smiles he gave, the thanks he uttered, the hugs he shared, and the stories he told as we gathered for dinner. In Philippians 2:4 (ESV) we are challenged to this:

> "Let each of you look not only to his own interests, but also to the interests of others."

Notice that it doesn't say we should *never* look to our own needs. Rather we should look to our own needs but *also* to the needs of others.

I got that verse lopsided for a long time. I pushed my own needs so far south that by the time I realized my error, I was too far down depression's road. What God is calling us to here is a healthy balance of caring for our own needs alongside the needs of others. When we do, we find that, in God's economy, this give-and-receive relationship benefits everyone involved.

I can't explain it completely, but I know it to be true. Something happens to our hearts when we serve others and allow our focus to shift outward. When we battle depression, it naturally turns us inward. By serving others, we force that inward focus to turn outward and allow healing and light to once again enter our darkened world.

That is why serving others is a vital step moving forward and it can even be a catalyst to finding healing and hope for our own hearts as we battle and overcome depression!

Avoiding the Comparison Trap

We might not like to talk about it, but the comparison trap is something we all have a tendency to fall into. I would certainly be remiss not to mention it before this book closes. I know very well how our thoughts can naturally spin that direction if we do not stay mindful. In fact, when I was battling through some of the worst of my depression, reading book after book about others overcoming, I thought maybe I was doing something wrong.

Why did it seem that they so easily traveled through this season when it felt like I was struggling for every breath and step? There were times I even got angry at God about it. It felt like what he did for them was not what he was doing for me. That's why, once again, I love this quote from Jon Acuff about the comparison trap:

> "Never compare your beginning to someone else's middle."

And it's so true. The comparison trap can really hinder your own personal progress. Instead of looking at what our next best step is, we sit and scroll through the lives of others, wishing we could be where they are at, all the while remaining stagnant in our own battle forward. We compare our beginning steps in this battle to someone who has been in the thick of it for much longer. We may be traveling a similar road, but our location on that road is unique. Theodore Roosevelt says this about comparison:

"Comparison is the thief of joy."

If we want to find our joy again, we've got to stop comparing ourselves to others. So how do we stop comparing?

1. Slow your scroll or stop scrolling altogether for a while. How many hours a day do you spend scrolling through other people's lives? How often do we sit there comparing the highlight reel of their lives to our own full-feature movie? Even if we were comparing, social media is not a fair assessment of anyone's life. Let's slow our scroll or even take a bit of a break from scrolling at all.

2. Remember that most people are facing a battle that no one else can see. We have a tendency to compare our inside battles to others' outward appearances. They may seem to have it all together, but the reality is that most people have insecurities, things they are worried about or battling with. Contrary to their outward appearance, they don't have it all together like you may perceive.

3. Start a practice of being grateful daily. A practice of gratitude can go a long way in helping us stop comparing our lives to others'. Every morning

during my meditation and prayer time, I write a gratitude in my simple journal. I try to make it very specific. Sometimes I really have to stretch to identify what I'm grateful for, particularly if it's been a rough week. But if we will dig for it, gratitude can be found every time.

4. Choose your heart attitude every day. Just like you have a choice about what you wear every day, you also have the ability to choose your own heart attitude. Every morning I ask myself, "what heart attitude will I choose today?" Sometimes it's patience. Sometimes it's the heart attitude of belief. Often, it's a heart attitude of trust. Trusting that today God has my steps planned out and all he is asking me to do is listen for his direction and trust him.

Betty Jamie Chung puts it together beautifully when she says, "Comparison with myself brings improvement, comparison with others brings discontent." So if you're going to compare, simply compare your next step to the one you took most recently. This battle with depression is truly marked by the steps you choose to take, not by everyone else's individual journeys.

The Best Next Step
Because each of our journeys is unique, everyone will take steps forward differently. The important part is that

we keep taking the next best step in front of us. That can be hard to do, especially when it seems like everyone else has a five-year plan while you're just hoping to get through the next week.

Now, don't misunderstand me. I think making plans for the future is important and mapping out what you would like to see happen in the next three to five years is a valuable strategy personally and professionally. However, remember that a three-to-five-year plan can never replace simply taking the next step.

The same concept has been true during my battle through depression, even though early on I struggled to understand it. I would talk to other people who had worked through their depression in what felt like weeks or months, not years like I had. (Do you hear that comparison voice starting to awaken?) I read all the books and tried to implement all the strategies and leap through the stages of the journey just as fast as they seemed to. My year one, year two, or even year three didn't look like theirs. What was I doing wrong?

In the early days of my depression, I battled the fog in my brain, making it feel near impossible to map out further than the week in front of me. As I got further in my journey, I found some clarity, but then the fog would roll in again. How was I supposed to make forward progress? How was I ever going to reach the other side of this depression?

Then one day I was hiking a mountain path. The trail twisted its way up and then down, around boulders and through meadows. It was a beautiful walk. Yet, there were still moments I had to stop and catch my breath.

It was in one of those pauses to catch my breath and rest my legs that I had this thought: My depression battle was much like hiking this trail. Twisting, turning, ups and downs. Some parts were a slow, tedious climb, while other parts of the trail offered a joyful rest from the uphill. But each beautiful and agonizing step led to one specific destination: the top of the mountain. The common denominator between the agony and the joy was taking the single next best step, not in skipping whole pieces of the trail. The only way I was going to scale this mountain was by taking the next best step in front of me.

And that is what I will say to you. Don't let the things in this book, from others, or from your own research paralyze your next step. Like I discovered at the beginning, there is no way we can see how all this will eventually play out. It's not that we can't make a plan or work to envision a healthier future, but our ongoing focus must simply be on taking our very best next step.

The next step is enough.

And, one day, you will look back and realize that you just climbed a mountain!

Final Words

As I wrap up this last chapter, here are some final things I want to remind you of:

✦ You are never, ever too broken to be loved. You have immeasurable value and, as such, are loved beyond what you can imagine by our Heavenly Father.

✦ You are no less of a Christian because you battle depression or anxiety.

✦ You always have a choice in how you are going to respond.

✦ No one else can do the work for you, but we can support you as you battle forward.

✦ Dig in with grit and take those first steps.

✦ Give grace to yourself and others.

✦ You never truly travel alone

✦ Have faith that Christ will help you win the battle.

Dare to fight—every day!

— *Victoria*

Your Turn

1. When you serve others, how does it make you feel? How could this be important to your healing and the depression you face?

2. As you look forward, who is someone you can serve in this next week?

3. As you finish reading this last chapter, what is the next step in your battle against depression?

4. What stood out to you about this week's reading? How might you apply it to your life this week?

This Week's Activity

What is one way you can serve someone else this week? Identify serving opportunities around you and then find a time to serve this week. After you serve someone else, take time to journal about the experience. How did it make you feel? What benefits did you receive? Is there another time coming up soon when you can serve again?

_____

For FREE access
to the following resources, visit:
www.victoriamininger.com

Heart Check-in Activity
Weekly Mood Tracker
Ideal Day Worksheet
Ideal Week Worksheet
Daily Rhythms Worksheet

About the Author

Victoria Mininger is a former pastor's wife, mom to four daughters and owns and runs a residential construction firm—Bear Creek Outdoor Living—and along with her husband and a team of craftsmen, they build cool stuff but more importantly they strive to build people. Victoria holds a bachelor's degree in psychology and Christian counseling from Liberty University with over twenty years of training and experience in Christian ministry. Victoria has spent the last few years facilitating depression support groups through the local church, desiring to see others find victory in their own journeys. In her downtime you can find her exploring and hiking the long trails of the Virginia Blue Ridge Mountains where she resides with her husband of twenty-four years and their four daughters.

Endnotes

i https://www.who.int/news-room/fact-sheets/detail/depression

ii https://www.psychiatry.org/patients-families/depression/what-is-depression

iii https://www.who.int/news-room/fact-sheets/detail/depression

iv https://www.health.harvard.edu/mind-and-mood/what-causes-depression

v https://www.health.harvard.edu/mind-and-mood/what-causes-depression

vi https://www.verywellmind.com/suicidal-ideation-380609

vii www.suicidepreventionlifeline.org

viii https://www.intouch.org/Read/Blog/the-purpose-of-god-s-word

ix https://fs.blog/2014/10/brene-brown-guilt-shame/

x Brown, Brené. *The Gifts of Imperfection*. Center City, Minnesota: Hazelden Publishing, 2010.

xi https://www.health.harvard.edu/mind-and-mood/exercise-is-an-all-natural-treatment-to-fight-depression

xii https://www.dictionary.com/browse/affirmation